No Wonder I Like Butterflies

My silhouette by Baron Scotford 1930 in my
Halidon House school uniform

No Wonder I Like Butterflies

A Life of Travel

Patricia Margaret

Book cover illustration by Margaret Irving Miller

Matador
9 Priory Business Park
Kibworth Beauchamp
Leicestershire LE8 0RX, UK
Tel: (+44) 116 279 2299
Fax: (+44) 116 279 2277
Email: books@troubador.co.uk
Web: www.troubador.co.uk/matador

ISBN 978 1783061 273

British Library Cataloguing in Publication Data.
A catalogue record for this book is available from the British Library.

Typeset by Troubador Publishing Ltd, Leicester, UK

Matador is an imprint of Troubador Publishing Ltd

Printed and bound in the UK by TJ International, Padstow, Cornwall

No Wonder I Like Butterflies

Most of my life I travelled
Often far and wide
Often staying for short times
In towns and cities and countryside
I sampled the tastes and smells of many exotic lands
I revelled in the vibrant colours
Of the markets, seas and coloured sands
I enjoyed each place for its unique style
But knew that I would move on in a short while

And so I watch this butterfly
Flit from bloom to bloom
Attracted by the colours and shapes
And the strong perfumes.
It rests for such a short time before it flutters off
Seeking out another blossom
Or a warm and sunny spot

And so it seems there are parallels
To my travel to foreign places
As I flittered around the globe
Seeking out new sights and scenes and different faces
It's no wonder I like butterflies.........

Written, on my behalf, by my daughter Sue.

For the many friends I have made along the way and for my late mother who kept all my letters.

But mainly for Sue and Liz and in memory of Peter.

Contents

Part One

Part Two

PART ONE

Chapter 1

Canvey Island, Richings Park and Fenwick,
Bond Street (1922-1939)

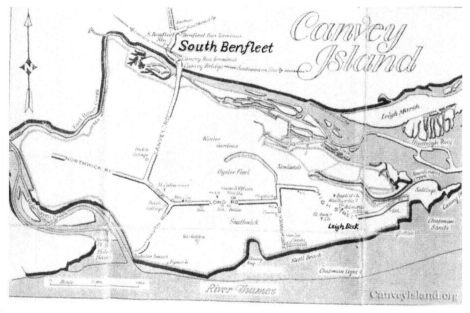

Map of Canvey Island

I would like to start at the beginning!

I was born on Canvey Island on 21st April 1922. Canvey Island is part of Essex on the northern side of the Thames estuary – so I am an Essex girl! Four years later, on the same date, but in very different circumstances the future Queen of England was born.

Across the Channel, later in the same year, in a private house in Antwerp, my future husband started his life. His mother, an English nurse, looked after a

Belgian interpreter during WW1. They married and lived in Antwerp for a while.

To get back to Canvey Island…not a very glamorous island as islands go but it does have an interesting history. The name Canvey comes from the Anglo-Saxon Cana. Historically this was a sheep grazing marshland which in later years supported a cheese making industry. Being low lying brought its problems of subsidence and flooding and in the 17C Dutch builders and engineers were employed to strengthen the sea defences and to reclaim land. Many of them settled and became part of the island's history.

My parents at the gate of Florence, the house where I was born

With my mother at 3 months old

I was born in 'The Florence' (the name, a legacy from the Dutch), a rented holiday home at Leigh Beck and I'm told that it was snowing! Leigh Beck was a settlement, now a town, in the SE corner of the island. My father worked in the City of London for the Royal Insurance Company, which meant catching a train from South Benfleet Station which was on the mainland. In order to reach the station he had to travel to the north of the island a distance of about 3 miles. I understand that the only transport was a horse-drawn bus and he then had to cross a channel of water. It was stepping stones at low tide; a rowing boat ferry at high tide! It was not until 1931 that a bridge, Colvin Bridge, was built and opened. There was a farm shop and a beach at Leigh Beck. It must have been very lonely for my mother, as I can't imagine many of the bungalows were occupied during the winter months. There was no electricity and water had to be collected from a standpipe.

Several times during the 18 and 19th centuries the island was submerged due to extensive flooding of the Thames. Sea defences were installed, but in 1953 serious floods hit the island again and caused 58 deaths. Unbeknown to me, (as by that time I was living in Jamaica), my cousin, Leo, who was in the army, was amongst the troops who were sent to help and reconstruct the sea walls. There are mud flats off the island and until 1957, when it was demolished, there was a hexagonal lighthouse which had been built in 1851 of iron. Called Chapman Lighthouse it is mentioned in Joseph Conrad's book 'Heart of Darkness'.

With my parents on my first bicycle

We left Canvey Island and lived in Sidcup and Surbiton until I was about 3. During those first three years there are photos which showed that we visited my aunt and uncle's house in Lancing in Sussex. Their house backed on to Broadwater and had steps down to the water and was called Tom Combleigh; the name being magnificently inscribed on a propeller above the front door. Another relation on my father's side whom we visited was his mother, my grandmother; the 'Mater' as she was called! She lived in Ember Lodge, Ember Lane in Esher with my eldest aunt called Edie. It was a 'being on best behaviour' occasion to visit Ember Lodge for afternoon tea. I never knew the 'Pater' as he had died in 1903. In fact he died at only 52 leaving my grandmother a widow for 38 years with 6 children....Edie, Herbert (my father who was known as Bert), Stan, Isobel, Geraldine and Gladys.

My grandfather had been a member of the Yeoman of the Guard, protectors of the monarchy, as opposed to Yeoman Warders who are the protectors of the Crown Jewels and the other contents of the Tower of London. My Aunt Edie was born at Kensington Barracks which was the home of the Yeomen.

My grandfather, Sawyer Ernest Spence, Yeoman of the Guard

Before we leave these early days, here is a coincidence, which actually dates back to before my parents were married. The following is an extract from a letter written by my mother to a magazine which was obviously featuring 'coincidences' at the time.

"When I was engaged, my fiancé Bert and his brother Stan went for a 10 days' walking tour in Devonshire. He gave me a list of the Post Offices he would call at each day for my letters. On his return he expressed disappointment that he had not received a letter from me; but I had written every day. A week later I received all my letters in one envelope with a covering letter from another man of the same name (H.Spence) who had been doing the same walking tour one day ahead! His letter contained an apology for opening and reading the letters with the excuse that although he realised they were not for him the first one was so interesting he couldn't resist reading all the others!"

My first memories, (or are these oft repeated stories that I think I remember?) are of playing on the back doorstep at our ground floor flat in Sidcup, balancing saucepan lids on their knobs. I remember being shut in a wardrobe for being a naughty girl. I also have recollections of being knocked down by a bicycle with a crowd gathering, and my mother being very cross because I had run into the road. Luckily I was not hurt.

When I was three, we moved to a brand new chalet bungalow on a new estate, Richings Park, near Iver in Buckinghamshire. This was definitely an 'up market' move, and I can remember the removal vans being unloaded, and being reunited with my toys! Here I had my own blue and white bedroom under the eaves at the top of the stairs, with a sloping ceiling. The back garden was quite large, tapering to a point, where I eventually had a swing, and my own little patch for 'growing things'! The bungalow was called 'Marigolds', and we had a circular flower bed in the front lawn, which, surprise, surprise, was filled with marigolds! I also had a favourite doll which I called Marigold. Even today, they are one of my favourite flowers, with their cheerful orange and yellow blooms. (Not the smelly French version (!) but, calendula.)

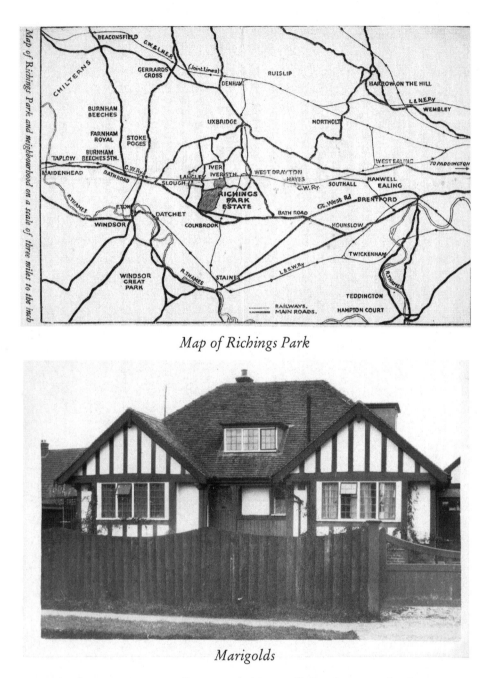

Map of Richings Park

Marigolds

I wonder how my parents discovered this small development in the country on the other side of London. Looking into the story behind this small estate, I found a very interesting tale of social history. The parkland, once owned by the first Earl of Bathurst, with a mansion built in 1700, was extremely fertile. Many literary figures, Alexander Pope, Thomas Gray, (of nearby Stoke Poges

8

fame with his Country Churchyard poem) and Joseph Addison, among them, were inspired by the wooded parkland and mansion. In more recent times the land was farmed by the Sykes brothers who came down from Yorkshire. Richings means rich meadows and they found some of the best soil in the country for growing crops. Unfortunately, cattle and horses grazing did not do so well, so eventually they bought Chantry Farm at Chute in Wiltshire.

Richings Park Estate was born soon after the end of the First World War. Brunel's Great Western Railway line ran to the north of the estate and Iver station was built and opened up in 1924. This was between the existing stations of West Drayton and Slough. The Sykes brothers founded the Richings Park Estate Ltd.

A post World War 1 scheme was introduced based on a 'no deposit' idea, where legal costs and other charges were added to the loan or mortgage to form an 'all in' monthly payment spread over 20yrs. It was realised the difficulty people had in saving for the initial deposit and how this prevented them getting on the 'housing ladder'. If only such schemes existed today! The range of houses and bungalows, initially 15 styles in all, presented an interesting selection. The costs ranged from £1.14 shillings a week to £3.3 shillings! Each house had a large front and back garden. The back gardens were big enough for a tennis court! They were well built and planned with 'fitted' kitchens. The emphasis was on providing facilities for local sports clubs and on encouraging everyone to join. It developed into a very friendly and social place to live.

When we first arrived in 1925, all this was still a long way from completion. The plan was for a triangle of roads with the houses backing on to a central recreation ground. Eventually the tennis courts and the cricket pitch were situated here, together with their respective club houses. Other roads were built around this area. Our bungalow was at the apex of the triangle and one of the first to be built. We were near the shops and the station, and there was also a cinema. I'm sure the shops gradually arrived but I remember the Estate Agents, a newsagent and confectioners, (more of that later) and a haberdashery, as some of the earliest.

My early childhood here was a normal happy one. My father was a leading light in the Hockey Club; he also played for the County of Bucks. My mother was a great walker and covered all the lanes and byways within an approx. 5 mile radius. This included such places as Stoke Poges, Black Park, Burnham Beeches, Eton, Windsor, Denham and of course Iver Heath and

Iver Village. As I got older, about 11 or 12, I cycled many of these routes on my own with no sense of danger; it was the normal thing to do!

I don't know how old I was, but one day I found a 6d. on the kitchen table and took it to the shop and bought some sweets. When my mother discovered what I had done she decided to teach me a lesson. She promptly escorted me back to the shop, where of course we were well known. I had to explain that I had stolen the sixpence and would they please let me return the sweets in exchange for the 6d! Taking the money and buying the sweets I do not remember, but I certainly remember the humiliation of returning them to the shop!

My mother enjoyed being a 'mum'. She knitted and sewed and played games with me as well as going on long walks. She was also very strict and kept a cane in the sideboard drawer which she did use on occasions, but I seem to have survived! One year she spent weeks collecting 'free samples' which were readily available and setting up little shops around the garden for my birthday party. Everyone had pretend money and it was a great success.

Whilst living at Richings Park my parents were friendly with Evelyn and Billy Mead. They remained family friends over the years and their daughter June and I went to the same school. At the beginning of the war I met up with Valerie and John, married friends of June. Soon we were all married and our families have kept in touch ever since, with each of us being godparents to each other's daughters and now two of us are mothers-in-law as well!!

This might be a good time to introduce some more of my family. I only remember odd incidences of meeting them when I was young. I have already mentioned 'the mater' and my father's siblings: the four sisters and his brother. Only my Uncle Stan had any children, and these, of course, were my cousins, two boys and a girl. All three cousins John, David and Geraldine were artistic in various ways. John was a head teacher and architecturally knowledgeable who lived in Cambridge and loved it. David was ingeniously artistic and Geraldine is a children's book illustrator. Her daughter, Lucy has followed suit and is the 'inventor' of 'Maisie the Mouse'.

Uncle Stan was in a gas attack during the First World War and suffered for the rest of his life. He was manager of the carpet dept. at the well-respected London Store 'Shoolbreds' in Tottenham Court Road and I remember visiting him there. My father also served in the army in WW1 and was stationed in Murmansk for a long time. He said this contributed to his early 'baldness' as in that permanently freezing weather he never took his hat off!

My mother had two sisters, one quite a bit older and one younger. She used to complain about having been the 'middle one'! The eldest sister, Rita, had three girls and a boy. The youngest sister, Hilda, always known as Lyn, who never married, joined the Land Army during the war and then 'disappeared' for many years. Eventually she was traced by the Salvation Army.

On my Aunt Lyn's bike [a 150cc Coventry Eagle]

Auntie Rita's eldest daughter, Peggy was a dancer, while Barbara and Sheila both eventually immigrated to Canada. Leo, the son, had a full time career in the Army. He now lives a couple of miles away from me in Dorset! This side of the family also is very gifted. Leo is adept at boat building, wood working, furniture making and ironwork. He married Rachael, who does woodcarving and creates wonderful flower arrangements. Their eldest son Tim, after 16 years in the army, became a cabinet maker. He now teaches 'bodging'; furniture making from green wood. Rupert, their younger son, is becoming a well-known contemporary artist, with a unique symbolistic and surrealistic style whilst Pippa, their daughter, is a water colourist and miniaturist.

This leaves me; an only child and an odd one out!!

To get back to Marigolds........

Up to this time I had attended the local 'kindergarten' on the estate. Then I graduated, with many others, to Halidon House School in Slough. We caught a train; a lovely noisy, smutty steam train! The school was just opposite the station. We had a green uniform blazer with a breast pocket badge of a water lily and the motto 'We Serve' embroidered underneath. We also wore a very strange hat, like a glengarry worn sideways on. One day my mother took me to London to visit Gamages a well-known department store, which eventually closed in 1972. It was famous for the toy department but also stocked a wide range of goods from car parts, pets and sporting goods as well as the more usual furnishings, carpets and fashion. Another attraction, at the time, was a kiosk where an American silhouettist named Baron Scotford, demonstrated his talents. In 1909 he cut the profile of Edward V11 and in 1930, amongst thousands of others, he cut mine! (see frontispiece)

Then, I don't know why, but at the age of 11, I was sent to 'board' at a school in Bexhill. Although I must have been there for about three years, I have very few recollections of those years. Bexhill at that time was full of girls boarding schools, and everywhere were crocodiles of uniformed girls going for 'walks'. Most notably was The Beehive, resplendent in their brown and yellow uniforms. For a while I couldn't recall how I got from Iver to Bexhill and back at the beginning and end of each term. We certainly didn't have a car. Then I remembered the 'school train'. The schools got together and booked a train from London. Each school was allocated so many carriages and the station was alive with uniformed girls, they were mostly girls, each searching for their group. Our school trunks had all been sent in advance and were waiting for us with all our clothing neatly labelled with Cash's name tapes. The uniform list included a garment called a 'liberty bodice' also navy blue knickers with white cotton linings. We had all the usual 'outer-wear' gymslips, skirts and blouses, blazers, indoor and outdoor shoes and a coat and hat. I learned the piano and passed my Grade 2 exam, and became a Girl Guide. I know this only because I have pieces of paper to prove it!!

GIRL GUIDES.

THIS IS TO CERTIFY

that you *Patricia Spence*

have been duly enrolled as a member of the Girl Guides
I trust you on your Honour to do your best to.
carry out the Guide Law at all times and to do a good
turn to somebody every day.

Date 20-6-34.

Baden Powell of Gilwell

Girl Guides Certificate 20th June 1934

Then my world fell apart the day the bailiffs arrived.

The humiliation and the circumstances were hard for me to take in. I was about twelve and obviously had no idea what had happened to lead to this event. It transpired that my father had been in debt and had 'borrowed' money from his office. It is not nice to have men invade the home and remove all the familiar furniture and possessions. I do remember my mother hiding a bedside rug she had made for me under the compost in the garden. It was of a sailing ship and had taken her hours to make. I can still visualize it, but have no idea what eventually happened to it.

My parents split up and my mother and I moved to a bed-sit in London, where she had to find a job to keep us. She had been a well-qualified secretary and soon found work, but it must have been so hard for her to return after 12 years of being at home. I was taken out of the boarding school and arrangements were made for me to weekly board at St Bernard's Convent in Langley and for my mother to pay a nominal fee of, I remember, 30 shillings a week, a sizeable chunk of what she was able to earn at the time. At weekends and school holidays I joined my mother in her one room in London. I slept wherever possible, for some time it was on two armchairs, with an old fashioned laundry basket pushed between them!

Front View of St Bernard's Convent with the Chapel on the left

St Bernard's was a good school and the nuns were kind, but strict. There were several day girls who lived locally, but as boarders our lives were very regulated, including having to attend daily mass. However, I enjoyed school. I played centre forward in hockey and attack in netball. Some of our teachers were nuns, but they were all female, all Catholic and mostly Irish. I had a 'crush' on our maths teacher (a Miss O'Callaghan) and consequently maths was one of my best subjects.

In my school uniform

We had midnight feasts on the landing above the imposing central staircase – some of the day girls supplying the ingredients! One night the usual entrance hall and corridor silence had ghostly sounds and shadows, as many of the nuns paced to and fro praying and rattling their rosaries. We discovered the next day that one of the community was seriously ill and the others were awaiting the arrival of a doctor.

During my stay at the Convent, the reigning King, King George V, who had been in bad health for a while, died on 20th January 1936. His funeral was arranged for 28th January in St George's Chapel, Windsor. As the school was nearby we were taken to join the assembled crowds to watch the procession from Windsor station to the Castle. Somehow I was separated from our group and was carried along by the crowd – a very frightening experience. King George V was succeeded by his eldest son Edward VIII who abdicated before the year was out. Somehow some of us managed to gather outside the staff room door and were able to listen to the abdication speech on their radio. His brother George VI then reluctantly succeeded him and reigned from 1936- 1952.

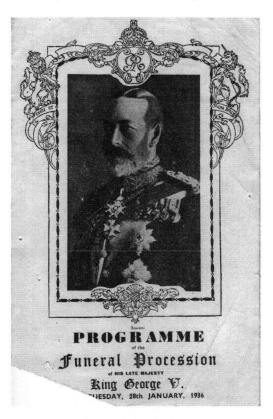

Souvenir programme of the Funeral Procession of King George V
Tuesday 28th January 1936

For the two years before the war my mother was secretary to the Women's League of Health and Beauty. This was a countrywide organisation and encouraged women to become healthy through exercising. The founder Mrs Bagot Stack, who died early in 1932, was succeeded by her daughter Prunella. She organised large displays of women exercising to music in perfect formations in their distinctive white blouses and black satin shorts, including one at Olympia for 5,000 women. My sixteenth birthday was during the Easter school holidays, the Thursday after Easter, and my mother and I were invited to the Bagot Stack's family home at 11, Holland Park for an evening's entertainment in honour of my birthday. This was provided by a group of Bavarian dancers in their lederhosen – very energetic with lots of leather slapping going on and all completely lost on a shy 16yr old! That same autumn Prunella married Lord David Douglas Hamilton. Several years later, when I was in the WAAF, I went on a PT Instructors course and the teacher was Pearl Hollick who had been a leading light in the Women's League.

In the summer holidays of the same year the school arranged for me to spend 2 weeks with a family in France to improve my French. Quite an experience travelling by myself across the Channel! They were kind people with a son and daughter around my age. They lived in Roubaix near Lille in a town house but we also drove to St Malo in Brittany for a week's holiday. There was a tennis match one day and both the players were English so I was asked to umpire! But I was not happy during my stay; I had no self-confidence. One day, when I was particularly miserable, I went for a walk by myself and took a self-photograph which I sent to my mother to show just how unhappy I was!

Some summer holidays I joined my father in a small hotel on the south coast, which was a somewhat strange existence! And sometimes I stayed with other friends or relatives. Eventually I left school with reasonable exam results, good enough for entrance to university but unfortunately with no chance of going to study architecture which had been my dream. It was immediately down to the 'labour exchange' to find a job.

By this time my mother had progressed to a flat in Canfield Gardens. To her credit she had repaid all the money borrowed (unbeknown to her), from friends and neighbours on the Richings Park estate. It transpired my father had been 'borrowing 'money to support our lifestyle. In those days husbands did not discuss money with their wives. They did not disclose how much they were earning they just allocated some 'housekeeping' money. Except that in our case, he did not give my Mother a regular amount, but just gave her what she wanted when she asked for it. So it was as much a surprise to her as me.

Anyway my first interview was for a clerk in a tea importer's office, accompanied by my mother, which was quite usual in those days. Talk about Dickens! It was a dark cubby hole at the top of a warehouse. No thank you! Then to Harrods as a sales assistant. Sorry – with my school certificate and good results, I was over qualified! Eventually I ended up in Fenwick in Bond Street; in those days a very expensive and exclusive store, like many in that part of London.

When living at Canfield Gardens and working at Fenwick I would occasionally walk all the way to work in order to save the bus fare. This was quite a long way but a pleasant enough route via Swiss Cottage along Avenue Road, Park Road past Regents Park and into Baker Street, from there to Oxford Street and eventually New Bond Street. Normally, however, I would travel by bus but taking care which stop I got on or off. There were fare stages and request stops and it was often worthwhile to walk to the next fare stage or get off a stage early to save a penny or two. Each bus had a conductor, most of whom, during the war, were women known as 'clippies'. They carried a rack of different coloured and priced tickets which they clipped at the appropriate stop. They carried a pouch for small change. They walked the length of the bus squeezing between standing passengers and up and down the stairs to get to the people sitting there. Front row upstairs had the best view and were popular seats. Another way of saving the odd penny or two was to go for lunch at one of the numerous Lyons Teashops where you would queue for a cup of tea and a currant bun. Then there were the 'posher' Lyons Corner Houses where there was a proper menu and usually a quartet or small orchestra playing popular music of the time. The waitresses were known as 'nippys' and were very smart in their little black dresses and white aprons and caps. I remember my mother taking me as a treat to a Corner House for lunch and truly embarrassing her and mystifying the waitress. I ordered some mashed potatoes and a mug of Bovril which I poured over the potatoes as a gravy. It was obviously my idea of heaven at that time!!

Anyway back to Fenwick. Here, behind the scenes, in a navy blue regulation dress, I started in the accounts department as a ledger clerk. The 'upmarket' shops in Oxford Street, Regent Street and Bond Street were quite intimidating to the casual customer. In Fenwick, an established family run business, each department had its own hierarchy dominated by the buyer. The most imposing of all was the 'Model' department. If, as occasionally happened, 'us' inferiors from the accounts department had a query to raise, we had to blend into the background until there was an opportune moment to approach this superior being! We had a back entrance, and were not allowed on the shop floor without special reason and were very low down on the social scale. I was promoted whilst there, within the accounts department, but because I was only 18 they refused to increase my salary. I was indignant and soon left.

However the world had changed soon after I had started this job as on Sunday 3rd September the nation was listening to the radio and to Neville Chamberlain's speech. "We are at war with Germany........" and very soon after the sirens went and all of us in London thought we were in for an immediate air raid, but soon the 'All Clear' sounded.

Chapter 2

ARP Warden & Pearn, Pollinger and Higham (1939-1941)

I became an Air Raid Warden with my friend Hilda. We both lived in the same terraced house that had been converted into flats in Canfield Gardens which was behind the store of John Barnes in Finchley Road. I lived on the top floor with my mother and Hilda lived with her sister, mother and her brother Jack, when he was on leave from the Navy, on the floor below. Our duty as wardens was to patrol the streets after dark to check no lights were showing. As soon as war was declared it was pitch dark at night, everyone had to buy or make black out curtains, no street lights were allowed and only low dipped headlights on any moving vehicles.

We really did have some 'peasouper' fogs; it was so easy to get lost or disorientated in the most familiar of streets, where vision was only a few paces. Buses often crawled along with someone with a torch leading the way, or they would be cancelled. We were issued with a tin hat, a stirrup pump and a bucket. With these we had to extinguish fires started by the many incendiary bombs being dropped at that time. In themselves they created very small fires, but the danger was when they fell on buildings with flammable contents. The ones that fell on the road were fairly easy, one of us would fill the bucket with water and the other would pump like mad! It was all a bit scary, with the sounds of bombs dropping in other areas and aircraft anti-guns firing away. An incendiary fell on the house next door, it penetrated the roof and burnt a path through all three floors down to the ground floor. Luckily the house was unoccupied at the time. I think we must have had help in extinguishing that one! Another scary night was when one fell through our roof and landed in the loft. My mother and I managed to get our loft door open and down flew a terrified blackbird which went berserk all around the flat. Since then I've had a horror of trapped birds. I remember my mother insisted, however tired we were, we always had to wash up and leave a tidy kitchen before going to bed in case we were bombed in the night.

On another occasion Hilda was having a bath (limited to 5in of water due to water rationing) when an incendiary fell in the street outside. She filled her bucket with bath water, stuffed a pair of knickers into her dressing gown pocket to put on when the opportunity arose and we dashed into the street. Having successfully managed to put the fire out she discovered the pants still in her pocket, never having had the opportunity to put them on! We fell about laughing! After many a disturbed night, we then had to get to work. Not always as easy as it sounds as we never knew where the bombs had fallen the previous night and which roads were closed and in fact whether one even had an office left to go to! Most mornings there were the remains of fires or even fires still burning and pavements covered with broken glass. If you eventually made it into work there was always the threat of more air raid sirens going during the day, when we had to go down to the air raid shelter in the basement.

When the war started everything went into 'basic' mode. There was a 'utility' range of furniture and also white china crockery with absolutely no embellishments. I decided to try and brighten things up. I found some water-proof enamel paints and 'decorated' the white china with a simple flower pattern. Surprisingly John Barnes, the store behind our flat, which was a subsidiary of John Lewis put them on sale!

It must have been mid-1940 when I started working for Mr Webb at the literary agency, Pearn, Pollinger and Higham of 39/40 Bedford Street, Strand. Bedford Street was in the heart of the literary area of West London, a busy and interesting environment of publishers, printers and booksellers. Their offices were on the upper floor, above those of The Lady magazine which is still there today. Ann Pearn, who was in charge of short stories and woman's magazines and an acquaintance of my mother, luckily got me a position.

Mr Webb was the Secretary of the company and responsible for all the legal contracts between authors and their publishers and for the general accounts. He had a little private office, but his secretary had to share a small room with, and keep an eye on, Olive and me. We were the general clerks and our job was to write up in large ledgers the terms of the contracts agreed between the authors and their publishers. Although I only worked there for about a year and was only a junior employee, the world of books, authors and publishers has fascinated me ever since. Authors would visit the office on occasions, many notable in their day. The Sitwell family were amongst some of the better known. Edith Sitwell was very eccentric; she would sweep in in a long black skirt and a wide brimmed hat, the very picture of an Edwardian lady! I don't remember seeing either Sacherveral or Osbert (her brothers) but they were on our books, as was the travel writer Rosita Forbes (Mrs Mc Grath) and the detective author John Dickson Carr (Carter Dickson) and many others whose works have long been out of print.

In the late 1950's the company split with Capt David Higham leading one agency and Laurence Pollinger and his son Gerald another. Laurence Pollinger's granddaughter, Lesley, now carries on the family business.

I had been 18 in April 1940 and knew that I was liable to be 'called up' and directed to work that was considered to be vital to the war. This included being drafted into any of the services or to a munitions factory, amongst other things. I was living and working in London and was a member of the A.R.P. (Air Raid Precaution) team in N.W. London, so I decided, rather than waiting to be 'drafted' I would volunteer for the WAAF (Women's Auxiliary Air Force). I went to Adastral House in Kingsway and signed the necessary papers. After waiting some time, I received my 'calling up' papers together with a rail voucher to report at RAF Innsworth near Gloucester on 18th April 1941 – three days before my 19th birthday. I can remember going to Paddington to join the train, crowded with dozens of very apprehensive girls, soon to be WAAFs.

Chapter 3

WAAF Middle Wallop (1941-1944)

Joining the WAAF

I am sure it must have been a shock to most recruits, but having been convent educated, from a single parent family with limited work experience – I was very naïve and unworldly to say the least. It was certainly a culture shock. Sleeping all together in a Nissan hut were recruits from all walks of life, daughters of titled families to prostitutes, school leavers to academics! Our bedding consisted of a mattress in three parts known as 'biscuits' which had to be 'stacked' each morning with blankets and bedding neatly folded on top. We were issued with our uniform of tunics, skirts, hat, tie, knickers, lisle stockings (with seams) and shoes. We were also presented with our 'irons': a knife, fork and spoon; a sewing kit called a 'housewife'; a button stick to protect our uniform whilst polishing our brass buttons; a belt buckle; a hat badge and finally a kitbag to transport our spare kit. On parade our shoes had to be shining and the seams in our stockings had to be straight up the back of our leg. We had frequent bed space and kit inspections.

We were each allocated a trade or occupation for our future service life. Somehow I was to become a Clerk (Special Duties) or 'plotter' which because of the Official Secrets Act was a bit of a mystery! Anyway before our specialist training we all had to do our spell at RAF Innsworth in Gloucester, of square bashing and learning to salute officers. One day we also lined up all day to have our 'jabs'- we received them all from plague to tetanus etc. (I think about 8/9 in total) in case we were posted overseas. We queued up alphabetically and as I was an 'S' it was evening before I received mine. Girls were fainting all over the place and some of us returned to our huts quite hysterical – we couldn't stop laughing!

Eventually we were 'passed out' and went for further training, which in my case was in Leighton Buzzard. Our accommodation here was an old building (previously a work house) with an outside iron staircase to reach the dormitory with its primitive washing conditions. Clerks (Special Duties) were divided into groups for the filter rooms, ops rooms and radar stations. I was to be an operations room plotter who received information from Radar Stations (then known as Radio Direction Finding) and Observer Groups personnel through a Filter Room. We displayed the information on a giant map with stands showing height, friend or foe, estimated number of aircraft and a magnetic arrow showing position and direction. These we controlled with croupier type rods. The controllers in the ops room then initiated fighter aircraft to scramble to attack the approaching bombers – air raid alerts – and other defence services.

On completing the course in May 1941 I was posted to RAF Middle Wallop. Back to the Nissan huts, which were on the other side of the road to the main camp, and with tin hats and gas masks always at the ready, I started duties at the ops room. This was in a commandeered private house – Wallop House in the neighbouring village. It had been totally mutilated, the ground floor being the main area with the large map etc and a part of the second floor removed to make a galleried area overlooking the 'plotting table'. We travelled by coach from the main airfield at the beginning and ending of each shift – working with only three watches of mainly WAAF – although we did have a few male colleagues. It was a tiring but exciting existence – trying to sleep during the day and all odd hours, while others on a different shift were awake; a challenge as we all slept in the same hut. We worked midday – 5pm; 11pm – 8am; 8am – midday then 24 hours off until midday the following day. Taking into account change-over time, travelling, eating, sleeping etc. it was no wonder we were all exhausted. We were free to leave camp on our 24hrs off, but had to get a special 'SOP' (sleeping out pass) to stay away from camp overnight, which was not always sanctioned! On our time off we tried to visit family and friends by hitchhiking – with hindsight a dubious means of transport, but everyone did it as there was little public transport and we couldn't have afforded it anyway.

With my colleagues at Hut 19, RAF Middle Wallop
[me standing in the doorway on the left]

With my colleagues at Hut 19 RAF, Middle Wallop [back row on the left]

One day I had accepted a lift on the A30 in an open top sports car, very posh, but unfortunately my passenger door hadn't been properly closed and it opened whilst we were travelling at speed and deposited me on the tarmac! I was very shaken but appeared to be alright. I was on my way to night duty and of course delayed shock hit me a few hours later and bruises appeared but I seemed to recover. I can still see the tarmac rushing by as I was falling out! Another time I had a lift in a RAF truck that had to deliver something to RAF Boscombe Down which was a very hush-hush site with special passes required. I was successfully hidden under a blanket on the floor of the back seat until mission accomplished and then we were under way again!

Our favourite pastime on our time off was to go to Salisbury on the camp bus and have tea at one of the numerous tea shops. Memorably – The Bay Tree and Stepping Stones, where everyone was rationed to one cake. We were always hungry and most of our pay, a very generous 1 shilling a day, went on extra food. Another destination was The Mount Café at Lopscombe Corner, when we either had to hitch a ride or cycle a long energetic up and down hill ride, but we were always rewarded with a 'fry-up'.

We were paid weekly at a 'pay parade' when the pay officer and his sidekick would set up a trestle table. We would all line up and come to the table one by one, say our name, service number (treble four, two double seven) followed by a smart salute and 'Sir' to be handed a small beige envelope containing our princely sum of a few shillings and pence.

Quite soon we moved to a custom built underground operations room, fashioned from an old quarry, at Over Wallop and I was promoted to Corporal and then Sergeant, which meant three chevron stripes on my jacket.

In my Sergeant's uniform

25

Another change came in our accommodation. A nearby large house known as Garlogs, on the road between Nether Wallop and Broughton was requisitioned. Our watch was billeted in this beautiful house, much to the distress of the owner a retired Major Jepson-Turner, who was downgraded to the gardener's cottage. June, who was my corporal and friend, and I used to visit him in his lowly cottage to try and cheer him up! In the front garden was a lake which was artificially frozen in pre-war Britain to enable his daughter, known as Belita, to practise her skating. Her mother, an American, after separating from Belita's father the major, took Belita to America before the war, where she became well known as a dancer as well as a skater; but he never saw her again. She died in 2005.

Garlogs, Middle Wallop

We were taken by coach from Garlogs to the new Ops Room and at the beginning of each shift I had to take a role call on the coach to make sure all were present. For the night shift of course, due to the blackout, I had to memorise the names alphabetically. I remember we had a Boon, Brown and Bunn, we also had a Black, Brown, Grey and White! It was all a bit pointless as anyone could answer and cover up a missing pal in the dark.

Garlogs' water supply was taken from a well and expected to meet the needs of up to 30 people. Suddenly there was this influx of WAAF personnel and it just couldn't cope. I and a few others became sick and were sent to the American Red Cross hospital at Odstock, near Salisbury. This hospital had been set up in 1942 and was a gift from John Harvard who shipped and assembled the huts on the site of the present day Salisbury General Hospital.

It was staffed by American Red Cross personnel. When we arrived we were put into rooms in the isolation ward and were diagnosed to be suffering from Sonne dysentery. Whilst in the 'isolation' ward I caught chicken pox, which must have been passed via the nurses, from a Squadron Leader in a nearby room. However it did cause a few eyebrows to be raised! My lasting memory, apart from the fact of how ill I felt, was seeing for the first time, boxes of tissues! Imported from the States and used lavishly by the staff; we had never seen anything like them.

During this time various things happened. I was seconded for a couple of weeks to RAF Worth Matravers – which consisted of a couple of huts on a cliff top near Swanage – mainly filled with 'boffins' – scientists who were working on radar and various defence and aircraft interception methods. There was a 'plotting map' and two of us were to interpret their findings in an experimental way. We were billeted in a B&B in Swanage, a luxury break from camp life, and transported daily to the very windy cliff top site. I was offered a commission which I turned down as the only vacancies at that time were in 'Equipment' which sounded very boring compared with working in the Ops room in the centre of things. Also we had more personnel and were able to change from 3 watches to 4. I was given D watch which consisted of 42 members. I have a record of this as on my 21st birthday I was given a beautiful home-made card containing all their signatures. I was also given – which I sadly no longer have – a very long scarf knitted in Air Force blue wool onto which everyone had embroidered their names in coloured silks.

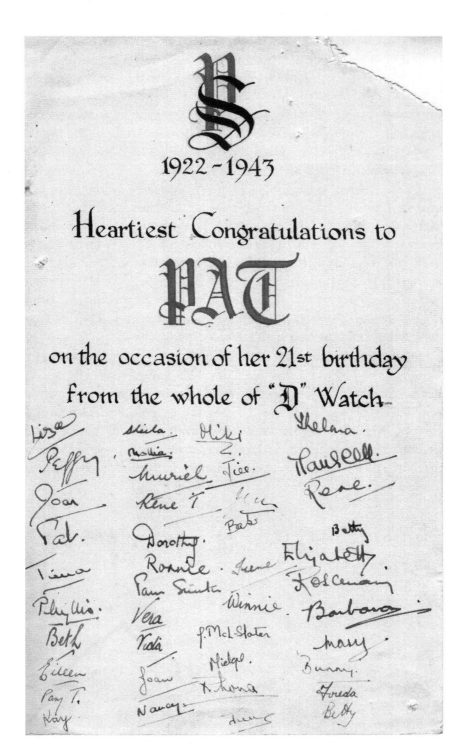

My 21st birthday card from D watch.

Also in 1943, I went to RAF Uxbridge for a PT instructor's course, where we participated in a grand display. So on my return there was another activity to fit into the working week – PT sessions!

W.A.A.F. PHYSICAL TRAINING COURSE, No. 29.
July, 1943.

WAAF Physical Training Course No29 July 1943
(second row down, third in from the right.)

A small group of the team waiting to perform [me at the far end]

There were numerous squadrons coming and going at the airfield, quite often two or more at a time, all part of Fighter Command and quite often specially trained night fighters. During 1941/43 the famous 604 Squadron was operating from Middle Wallop. The 604 Squadron leader was the well-known Flight Lt (later Group Captain) Cunningham – Cat's Eyes Cunningham – after his ability to shoot down enemy fighters in the dark, and after whom the 'cat's eyes' lights in the centre of country roads were named. Actually the improved facility for shooting down enemy aircraft at night was due to the improvement in RADAR equipment, but the story was put around that it was due to the consumption of carrots which improved 'night vision'! The squadron originally flew Blenheim aircraft but was later equipped with Mosquitoes which were built of wood and a very efficient night flying aircraft. We had a viewing gallery in the Ops Room which he visited one day to see the set up.

The Operations Room at RAF Middle Wallop
[me standing in the middle at the back on the telephone]
[with kind permission of the RAF Air Defence Radar Museum
NEDAD. 2002.112]

After a while my accommodation was moved back to the main camp where I was able to use the sergeants' mess. There were less than half a dozen WAAF sergeants and I think probably only one of those apart from me used it; it was an intimidating place to enter! Because I often came off night duty about the same time as the aircrews were returning from their night flying missions – I somehow became entitled to a 'night flying breakfast'; a special fry-up which was much appreciated. With this privilege I became an onlooker on the returning night-flying crews. They were exhausted after flying, attacking and evading the enemy aircraft. They were debriefed before arriving in the mess where their mixed emotions were palpable. The adrenaline fuelled banter and jokes mixed with anxiety and sadness for those missing or known to have crashed. They lived on the edge, in a world of their own; very brave young men, a few of whom I got to know a little. There was a Link Trainer on the airfield used by the pilots to practice their skills. The Link Trainer instructor was a sergeant with whom I got friendly and I used to unofficially have a little 'flight'. It was a convenient sanctuary to retreat to and have a very innocent little cuddle! Unfortunately he was posted and we soon lost track.

After I moved to living back on the main airfield I was issued with a bike to go to and from the Ops room. It was an uphill ride on the return and I was known to fall asleep on my bike on returning after a night shift and land up in the hedge!

Being in the forces and with the Official Secrets Act, you knew nothing of the country-wide picture of the progress of the war – we were so involved with our little part of it. However you could not but be aware that something was afoot at the beginning of June 1944. The camp was adjacent to Salisbury Plain, where numerous army camps were based. Gradually all the roads became solid with convoys heading south and then the skies became almost black with aircraft with the sound of overflying heavily laden bombers. The ops room table was covered with aircraft movements; a busy and exciting time.

Chapter 4

WAAF Orkneys (1944-1946)

Later that year I was posted to the Orkney Islands as it was feared that German troops based in Norway would now mount an attack. It was quite a journey to reach the airfield at Grimsetter near Kirkwall the capital of the Orkneys. Together with many others, I joined the troop train in London complete with my worldly possessions in a kit bag and a few sandwiches for the 24hr journey to Thurso. The train was packed, mainly with the army travelling north, and to start with the only vacant places were in corridors with everyone sitting on their kit bags. We rumbled on through the night to see thick snow the further north we went. Eventually we arrived at Thurso and had to board a vessel, the Earl of Zetland, at nearby Scrabster, a flat-bottomed boat on which we rode the extremely rough crossing of the Pentland Firth. This crossing could take from 5 – 8 hours depending on the weather conditions. We passed by the Old Man of Hoy and eventually landed at Stromness.

The only passengers on board were members of the armed services and residents of the Orkneys. Visitors were not allowed access to the islands during the war. There were very few females on board and most of the men appeared to be bad sailors with resulting consequences!!! Luckily I love a rough sea and whilst others were miserably being seasick above and below deck I relished the open air and the exhilaration of the movement on deck. On arrival at Stromness we were taken to RAF Grimsetter (known to us in the services as RAF Grim'ster, the location being so barren and bleak) which was some distance across the mainland island to the east of the capital Kirkwall. The ops room was in an ugly block of a building and our accommodation was in huts. On wet and windy wintry nights it was a damp and miserable walk. In winter it was dark for about 20 hrs, cold but not extreme but very, very windy with the added plus of the Aurora Borealis giving a spectacular display. Summer months were light most of the time.

The Orkneys are a fascinating group of islands with a history that can be traced through its many remains and ruins of ancient times. The locals were farmers mostly and the islands are dotted with stone crofts, some large some small. Farming was a family concern with the women giving a hand on the land as well as being excellent cooks. Before the Second World War, there were many inhabitants of the Orkney Islands who had never been across the sea even to the mainland of Scotland. Many have still not left their little family crofts and many never will. They have never seen a train or a double-decker bus.

Kirkwall is the largest town on the largest island and is the capital of the Orkneys. So we will start our tour of this group of islands at Kirkwall itself. It is a city of the past and there are many reminders of ancient days and the people who lived here. The buildings are all of stone and are strong and solid to withstand the strong gales of winter and the streets are narrow and cobbled. Broad Street is the main thoroughfare of the town, but inspite of its name there is only room for one car to pass and there are no pavements. Nothing is regular; some buildings jut out into the street. Arriving by steamer, passengers on deck would be struck by the silhouette of the cathedral which stands out above the town and is built of red sandstone. You get a full length view of this simple but magnificent building with a square tower surmounted by a spire. This is a relic left by the Norse Earls of Orkney in the 12ᵗʰ century.

Kirwall harbour is small and full of little fishing craft and on the foreshore stands the Kirkwall Hotel. This meeting place of the elite was as well-equipped and with standards as high as any hotel of equal size in more populated parts. There were a variety of shops from the 'village' shop at one end of the town selling vegetables, groceries, homemade bread, cookies and big round cheeses straight from the farm, to newsagents selling newspapers delivered by air and which didn't arrive until late in the day. During bad weather Orkadians remained blissfully unaware of outside happenings apart from those who listened to the BBC news. Continuing down Broad Street one passed drapers, the Bank house and the little coffee shop with an upstairs tea room where during the war they served drop scones and pancakes with lashings of fresh butter. This was a popular spot with many of the forces stationed nearby. From the window of this upstairs room you looked across the narrowest part of Broad Street where a car could hardly pass. A little further down was Kirkwall's only cinema the Albert Kinema, recently destroyed by fire.

A continuing theme seemed to be that we were always hungry. We used to visit neighbouring farms to buy eggs and occasionally we were lucky enough to get some of the famous Orkney cheese. A wonderful family living in Kirkwall were very good to us. They had open house to any Officers and NCOs (Non Commissioned Officers) from the nearby airfield. We had transport laid on for visits to Kirkwall, which consisted of climbing into the back of a large lorry and sitting precariously on benches or just standing and hanging on to anything available! John and Betty Dickson and their daughter Elizabeth lived above the bank in Bank House as John was the manager of The Royal Bank of Scotland. They always had a lovely warm fire on winter evenings and a tinful of homemade biscuits and cakes to welcome us. Many a friendship was formed in their comfortable sitting room.

John, Betty and Elizabeth Dickson, Kirkwall

I remember one day walking south across open country, (about a 6 mile round trip) to reach Scapa Flow and saw the mast of the sunken Royal Oak. Scapa Flow was considered a safe anchorage for naval ships, but early in the war (1939) a very daring and clever trip by a German submarine navigated the defences of the Eastern entrance. The channels between the islands were protected by sunken ships and presumed impenetrable by U boats, so this was a devastating blow to the Royal Navy and led to the building of the Churchill barriers between the islands – concrete blocks piled high and topped by an open road. There were four in all connecting the mainland to Lamb Holm, Glimps Holm, Burray and finally South Ronaldsay.

One day one of the pilots from the Sergeant's mess had to make a journey to Sumburgh which was the airfield on the southern tip of the Shetland Islands, a rather scary airfield as the peninsula is very narrow and the East/West runway went from coast to coast. There was also a North/South runway. Very unofficially I went with him as a passenger in the Rapide bi-plane; it was to be a quick up and back. However, it didn't actually work out like that as the weather unexpectedly closed in and we couldn't return that day. This meant we had to travel to Lerwick, the capital, to spend the night. It was 25miles north along a road following the Eastern coast and, as we were informed, containing 33 hairpin bends; and all this in the black out! I gather that this road was only improved in the 1990's. When we eventually reached Lerwick I was a problem! Bob could stay in the Sgt's mess but there was no accommodation for WAAF Sgts! Eventually I was found a bed in a hut of female volunteers; I think they were from the WRVS.

I had another unofficial trip in the same aircraft when returning after some leave. To avoid the awful train journey I somehow managed to hitch a lift. We took off from Woodley airfield near Reading and I 'navigated' from an open cockpit following roads and railway lines. As far as I can remember we went to Inverness and took the train from there.

I was 'released' from the WAAF on 28th Feb 1946 and received my final payment of 6/10d a day (about £2.10s a week)! After nearly five years spent in the WAAF, I was about to start afresh. I was to spend a similar amount of time working for BOAC which culminated in my marriage. This was followed by 25 years of being an expatriate wife and all that that entails, followed by a further 30 odd years of on-going and busy retirement.

Chapter 5

BOAC UK and Egypt (1946-1949)

On my release from the WAAF I went to Southbourne to join my mother who had a small flat on the cliff-top near to Hengistbury Head. From here I joined BOAC. BOAC started operating from Hurn airport, Bournemouth, in April 1946 and must have been advertising for staff. 'Number 2' line was based at Hurn and operated converted RAF York and Lancaster aircrafts. I worked in the engineering department on statistical charts. These recorded man hours spent on maintenance, engine life etc. I was very proud of my 'wall' of neat charts. I even had an assistant. The manager of 2 Line was Cecil Rhodes whose son Geoff later worked for Peter and then Sue (our daughter) worked for him on various postings abroad and they are still friends today.

Engineering Statistical Charts, No. 2 Line Hurn 1946 [me standing]

A York aircraft operating out of Hurn. This aircraft [G-AGNT] was used to operate the joint inaugural BOAC/South African Airways Springbok service on the 10th November 1945. The routing was Hurn – Castel Benito – Cairo – Khartoum – Nairobi – Johannesburg

In February 1947 I transferred to Heathrow, which was in its infancy, as a check-in clerk. Arriving and departing passengers were 'handled' in huts on the North side of the airport. Female passengers' weight was averaged at 65kg, male at 75kg and the baggage allowance was 30kgs. This information appeared on an APS (Aircraft Prepared for Service) form and seating and luggage details were calculated to get the C of G (centre of gravity) right for take-off.

I lived in various bed-sits near the airport at West Drayton, Osterley etc. Most 'unmarrieds' started their working lives in bed-sits which were very numerous in London and the suburbs. But very typical of that time, when you arrived at the front door of the house containing the vacant room, was a notice saying, "NO BLACKS – NO IRISH – NO DOGS."

I then transferred to working in the headquarters at Speedbird House at Brentford on the Great West Road and rented a flat nearby. It was the upstairs of a private house in 'The Ride', Brentford and I was able to walk to work. Speedbird House was a very impressive Art Deco building with a grand entrance complete with waterfall. (This later became Beecham House; the head office for Beecham; the company who Liz, our younger daughter, worked for, for many years.) My job description however was not so grand. I was an assistant to the assistant to the Manager of Africa and Middle East

Area! The hub of which was Cairo where there was a large set-up and BOAC were agents to Aden Airways, East African Airways, QANTAS etc. It was interesting working at Head Office and very good for my knowledge and the geography of that part of the world. I remember the manager's claim to fame was that, whilst in the army in charge of Italian POWs, he had ended a hunger strike by the inmates by lining them up outside the cookhouse and getting the cooks to fry onions until they could no longer resist the tempting smell!

After Brentford I was sent on a course at Aldermaston. This was very strange as it was supposed to be a course for airport managers. On the course were some real old time managers who had their own established empires at strategic airports around the world Karachi, Calcutta, Rangoon, the Middle East, Bermuda and such stations. There must have been about a dozen of them and then Jeanne and myself. We were a lot younger and had hardly any experience! Ironically, and showing the farce of such courses, but maybe because I had a younger brain- I came top of the class with 93%...and Jeanne did well too!

As a result of this, we were both sent on a short overseas posting to Cairo. We were meant to stay for 6 months but I ended up being there 9 months; the most amazing experience of my life up until then.

Picked from sixty girls as the two brightest and smartest BOAC air receptionists at London Airport, Pat Spence, 26 (left), of Bournemouth, and Jean Cox, 27, of Beckenham (Kent) have been rewarded with a six-month winter tour of duty in Cairo.

A press cutting from The Mirror [with kind permission of Mirrorpix]

With Jeanne prior to our posting to Cairo 1948
[with kind permission of Mirrorpix]

In September 1948 I left a war-torn Britain, rationed and restricted in so many ways. Flying was for the wealthy, the well-known and 'upper class'!!!

Having spent the night before in a hotel, I left Southampton on a Solent Flying boat. The cabins were fitted with four lounge seats with a fixed table in between and there was only one 'service' – first class. Luckily there was another staff member on board, a steward who was repositioning, who was travelling as a supernumerary crew. We flew to and landed on the lake of Marignane which was the station near Aix-en-Provence and then night-stopped again at the same hotel where Churchill stayed! Talk about being a bit out of my depth!! Flying boats were daylight only flyers and every night was spent in a first-class hotel. I don't remember much except that I was more than a little awe-inspired by the opulence of it all.

The next day we flew to Sicily and landed at Augusta for refuelling. Here I do remember the wonderful blue of the Mediterranean and the transit lounge where there were huge bunches of grapes lying on blocks of ice in the centre of the tables. From here to Egypt – a wonderful view from the air of the narrow fertile strip bordering the Nile and the uninterrupted expanses of sand dotted with minute spots of green oasis. We saw the Pyramids and the Sphinx and then down to earth or rather down to the murky waters of the Nile and the noise, heat and smells of the slums of Cairo. We landed at Rod-el-Farag an area north of the city. I felt very alone as I was taken by a Company car on the long drive through the city to the suburb of Heliopolis – up the sweep of the drive to the grand entrance of the Heliopolis Palace Hotel (H.P.H.).

Postcard of the Heliopolis Palace Hotel, Cairo 1948

The hotel had a very imposing foyer and beyond this a huge lounge with, what was reputed to be, the largest one-piece carpet in the world, with dozens of armchairs and settees lost in the large expanse. The ceiling was extremely high and was inhabited by bats which would occasionally swoop down and scare the living daylights out of me. Beyond this was a semicircular glass-enclosed dining room with columns supporting the ceiling. I was soon to become very familiar with these surroundings as my job was to run the airline office in the hotel itself. This consisted of a large open area where we had a reception desk, a cashiers' counter and several chairs for callers. The staff consisted of three male cashiers, five female receptionists, two messengers and a dragoman. The cashiers and receptionists worked in shifts. At this time there was an Arab-Israeli war going on and all the cashiers were Jewish members of staff who were not allowed to work at the airport; the girls were various nationalities.

My office in the Heliopolis Palace Hotel, Cairo 1948 [me seated]

In Cairo, being very cosmopolitan, everyone spoke at least Arabic, French and English (generally a mixture of all three, whichever word came to mind first!) and usually, in addition, Greek, Turkish and German. The two messengers were Egyptian, complete with their red tarbooshes and black tassels. Abdullah, the dragoman, also wore a tarboosh. He was the local guide and took passengers around the Pyramids and down to Memphis and Sakkara.

This was the day of the Lockheed Constellation aircraft "the Connies" and Cairo was the thriving hub of air routes and airlines from all over Africa and the Middle East, in fact, world-wide. It was a transit centre and the

41

Regional Headquarters of the African and Middle East Region.

We were extremely busy, changing currency, traveller's cheques, dealing with onward bookings, transit passengers, endless enquiries from night-stopping passengers and of course, the inevitable delays. In those days an engine change could take at least 5 days!

We had a block of rooms permanently booked for the airline. We had crews and passengers not only from our own company, but also from other airlines for which we acted as agents – notably QANTAS and Aden Airways. There was no division of classes on the aircraft as everyone was a 'first-class' passenger and even on land based aircraft, as opposed to the flying boats, night stops were scheduled during long flights, such as the London-Australia journey. Practically every day therefore, Abdullah would take at least one party on a sight-seeing trip. In those days the Pyramids really were on the edge of the desert – about 5 miles from town- with one hotel, the Mena House, for those wishing to stay and see the moon rise over this spectacular setting.

A visit to the Pyramids [from right to left, me, Jeanne Cox, Peter Kirwan, Vicki U'Ren and another colleague from the office]

Abdullah lived on the Old Pyramid Road. I vividly remember a party he invited some of us to. There was the beating of the drums, the naked flames of the lamps and dancing to the rhythmic thumping on the warm skins on the drumheads. Abdullah and his friends in their galabeihs and fezes – the dancer with an earthenware jar of water balanced on his head, gyrating faster and faster – and me being the only female there! I was lucky enough to go on a few trips with Abdullah and the passengers. I saw the Sphinx at Memphis and the step pyramid at Sakkara.

This was the time of King Farouk and his excesses; the extremely rich and the very poor. One day at the H.P.H. there was a fencing contest to which the King was coming. Prior to his arrival the large entrance foyer was cleared except for his armed soldiers on guard. Various guests, staff etc. Vicki and myself included, were kept to the sides but, nevertheless, we could see, when in a hushed silence Farouk arrived hardly visible amongst a block of bodyguards. It really was deathly quiet when suddenly there was a crash by me – the noise exaggerated in the unnatural stillness – it came from where Vicki and I were standing – all the guns swung in our direction and then the tenseness relaxed – the handle of the handbag that Vicki had been holding had broken and the bag had fallen to the ground! These handbags, by the way, were considered a good buy. They came from a shop called King Tut, in a range of colours; mostly a box-like design made in leather and costing about two pounds. I had a dark green one which was later stolen on a London underground – but that is another story!

The streets of Heliopolis were always busy in the mornings and evenings when the shops were open and business was carried out. Afternoons were for siestas. Bright little Arab paper-sellers aged 9 or 10 with a range of newspapers from many countries would accost you, always offering you the paper in the correct language. They knew exactly everyone's nationality and prided themselves on their skill, especially as it was a truly cosmopolitan place.

Amongst the many smells, mostly and indescribably "Middle East", was the lovely perfume at evening time of jasmine. Small boys would thread the blossoms together into a spike and sell them for a piaster or two and the soundtrack of the open air cinema would blaze across the nearby streets.

This was also the day of the Pasha, the idle wealthy gentlemen in their flowing robes who would gather in groups and sit for hours gossiping over one cup of Turkish coffee and a glass of water. Turkish coffee is served in small cups; very thick and very sweet.

A typical street coffee seller, Cairo

After the first few nights staying in the luxury of the Hotel, I moved into a pension – the Villa Montrose – and then to a bachelor's flat on the roof of the Roxy building. Here I was self-contained and I loved my little home. Every day I walked to the Hotel where I changed into the very unflattering uniform then provided, of heavy khaki drill, with metal military buttons and buckle which had to be cleaned with a button stick – shades of my days in the WAAF! Because of the Arab-Israeli war going on the situation was so tense that we were not allowed to wear any uniform on the streets.

I had a paraffin cooker and an ice box in my kitchen. The latter was literally a box in which you put a block of ice, which lasted about a day. A little girl used to climb the stairs every morning to my flat at the top of the building and deliver my block wrapped up in a piece of sacking.

My 'ice girl'

During my stay in Cairo Jeanne and I took the night train to Luxor for the weekend, as one does! The flying boats landed there for refuelling and there were two or three contract staff, one of whom was Peter who had come down from Cairo. The place was full of contrasts. There was the luxury of the Winter Palace Hotel, which overlooked the Nile, while the majority of the local Egyptians lived in the dusty backstreets of Luxor. Jeanne and I went up to the roof of the Winter Palace Hotel to watch Peter 'talk down' a couple of flying boats as they landed on the Nile below us.

Peter on the roof of the Winter Palace Hotel in Luxor 'talking down' a flying boat as it landed on the Nile.

When the flying boat landed the passengers transferred to a motor launch which took them ashore. In 1949, the grand Winter Palace Hotel catered for the very few and very wealthy visitors to the Luxor Temple and the Valley of the Kings. Jeanne and I stayed at the smaller Luxor Hotel. We were taken to a deserted Karnak Temple accompanied by our own personal guide. The area was still very primitive with dusty, sandy 'roads', locals riding donkeys and of course it was very hot. We crossed the Nile on a felucca, the local sailing boat – Jeanne, me and one of the other staff. We were to be met on the western bank by a car, there being so few visitors at the time that this was a sufficient mode of transport to take tourists to the tombs. We were the only ones being shown around 'King Tut's' tomb and the village of the workers. We were in the Valley of the Kings, a hot, dusty, magical place.

The Luxor Hotel (1949)

With Jeanne in the gardens of the Luxor Hotel (1949)

At the temple of Karnak with a local guide

Our Visit to the West Bank and the Valley of The Kings.
This was the visitor's transport

Chapter 6

BOAC Air Stewardess (1949-1951)

*Traffic clerks sunning themselves outside the huts
at Northside, Heathrow 1949*

On my return from Cairo in May 1949 I started working on shifts at passenger departures and arrivals at Northside Heathrow, which consisted of a series of huts. Vacancies were being advertised for stewardesses so I applied and found myself on a course at Cranebank, near the airport. We had a 'mock-up' cabin and practised 'silver service' by serving bottle tops and pieces of cardboard and also learnt how to carry several plates at once! We learnt how to use the Crittal ovens in the small galley where everything had its own tightly fitting space and tricks of the trade such as adding a small amount of salt to a pot of coffee at altitude improved the taste! There were printed menus for each passenger and all meals were served 'silver service' from a trolley. There were separate ladies and gents loos on board, each supplied with complimentary toiletries. Elizabeth Arden supplied the bottles for the ladies and we were sent to their training school for a day to learn about their products. There was even room for a nappy changing shelf. We were also sent to a swimming pool for 'ditching' training. We had talks on first aid and how to cope with air sickness, fainting etc. Luckily I never had to cope with a birth or death on board but on occasions had to make the tannoy announcement: – "Is there a doctor on board?" Contrary to the perceived legend I was not a trained nurse and did not speak 3 languages – just a little French and a smattering of basic Arabic and Spanish!

PATRICIA O'BRIEN spends a day in the sky and says:

GLAMOUR?—NO ... but it's one job in five thousand

DID you ever picture yourself in the uniform of an Air Hostess, smiling graciously at rich and handsome passengers? If you are female and under fifty you probably have, at some time or other.

Commercial airlines have a steady influx of applications from would-be hostesses. And, apart from the thousands that actually do apply there are many more who go wistfully to their type-writers or shop counters, dreaming of a life in the sky.

For every air job available the supply exceeds the demand by something like five thousand to one .... not a very encouraging ratio.

Very few girls who apply for the job have any idea what it entails. To find out I accompanied a B.O.A.C. hostess on a day's work aloft over the Atlantic. Even the term hostess is considered rather old-fashioned now.

The girls are stewardesses. And to become stewardesses they must be between the ages of twenty-one and thirty. They are not usually shorter than 5ft. 3in., or taller than 5ft. 7in. And their weight must be reasonable! Their eyesight must be perfect, they must pass rigid health tests, must have a good second-ary education. They must be attractive, have pleasant personalities (that means abundant patience and tact) and speak at least one other European language, preferably French.

A successful candidate goes to the B.O.A.C. school for eleven weeks. Her training includes catering, service of food and drink, first aid, use of oxygen in aircraft, route geography, care of equipment. Psychology, fire precaution, and valet technique are tossed in for good measure.

WITH all this behind her the trained stewardess takes to the air. Queen of all she surveys?—not much! She is the most junior member of the air crew.

Now for her day's work. She's flying to New York! Wonderful . . . but it isn't quite as simple as all that. She reports at the airport on the previous day, with a small suitcase carrying her needs for a range of possible destinations, from Iceland to Bermuda.

She moves into the nearby B.O.A.C. hostel and is on call duty.

With the second steward, she checks food and equip-ment from the catering stores to the aircraft.

Then she goes back to the hostel, still on call, and shows up again the next evening for her flight.

Her first duty is to greet the passengers as they board the plane, help them with their hand luggage, see that their safety belts are fastened, supply them with glucose barley, and answer their questions.

She's too busy to work up friendships—and she's not constantly being plied with invitations when the des-tination is reached.

It happens sometimes, but not very often. These passengers are preoccupied, and some of them may be tired and a little grumpy.

ON our trip, several passengers were airsick. A special formula had to be mixed for a baby . . . a queru-lous old woman demanded coffee every hour on the hour. The two stewards and one stewardess served a three-course dinner to forty-five people, with speed and efficiency.

While the passengers settled down to sleep our stewardess filled in their landing and Customs papers for them. She was on call all night, bright and efficient, with not a hair out of place.

After a day in New York she will probably proceed to Bermuda. Travel . . . sure, it's wonderful, but so many changes of climate might well give her pneumonia if her constitution wasn't tops.

You might say that uniforms save on a girl's cloth-ing budget, but stewardesses need many more clothes than their earthbound sisters. Snow boots for Canada . . . cottons for Bermuda. Date dresses for their shore leave are crammed in and out of suitcases, pressed, and re-pressed so often that their life expectancy is cut by half.

THERE is quite a high incidence of wedding bells, but after all, considering the age group and the qualifi-cations these girls have, marriage does seem inevitable. Mostly it is in spite of, rather than because of, their jobs. They can't plan a theatre date in London, for instance, when they might well be in Iceland or Austra-lia when the time comes around.

And the future in the job? None. When she is past the required age she could be transferred to a ground job—but none of them can regard that prospect as appetising.

It's a difficult job, a tedious and sometimes exciting job, but each girl loves it—because she is one in five thousand.

Press cutting from The Mirror 9th January 1950 extolling the virtues of life as a Stewardess[with kind permission of Mirrorpix].

In November 1949 I went on my first trip. It was a freighter operating across the Atlantic and I was on my own catering for the crew, which included a very 'anti-female' prejudiced Captain! He made me fry sausages, which had obviously gone off, for their breakfast before I was allowed to throw them away!

I can't remember where we stopped and refuelled on that particular flight, but because of the prevailing westerly winds and the limitations of fuel capacity, most journeys originating in the UK needed an additional stop or two for refuelling. Flying on the Northern Atlantic routes frequently entailed a stop at Prestwick, then Iceland and/or Gander in Newfoundland. Keflavik, the airport at Iceland, was often covered in snow and the runway outlined by 'Christmas trees'. I remember that alcohol was plentiful but also very expensive. Travelling on to Gander made a long and tiring flight and although the cabin crew had no limit on their flying hours, the flight crew did. In the 1950's Gander was one of the busiest airports in the world, although conditions for stopovers were fairly basic.

Shannon, in the south of Ireland, was a popular stop for the Southern Atlantic routes, made even more popular in 1951 when the first duty free shop in the world was opened. The aircraft would then make an additional stop at the Azores, a group of islands owned by the Portuguese. The airport on Santa Maria was built by the Americans in order to maintain supply lines between America and Europe during the Second World War, but became a useful re-fuelling stop for commercial aircraft after the war. The islands enjoyed a rural way of life with small, low rise homes and horse and carriages and bullock carts being the main modes of transport.

Bullock carts in The Azores

When we were scheduled for a flight we had to check in the day before and were taken by coach to Dormy House in Sunningdale and we were on 'standby' until we were taken to the airport the next day for our flight. Prior to departure we had to check all the catering and bar facilities on board for the flight as well as life jackets, oxygen masks etc.

My first passenger flight was a training trip accompanying another stewardess in December 1949 over Christmas to New York. The cabin crew consisted of a chief steward, a bar steward and the stewardess who I was shadowing. 'Up front' were a Captain, First Officer, Flight Engineer, Radio Officer and Navigator. Conditions on the flight deck were very cramped and primitive in comparison to the facilities today. They were all working manually and had to cope with the changing conditions so well described in David Beaty's books. The weather on this flight was terrible and we stopped several times before eventually landing at Boston, where, exhausted as we were, we had to accompany our passengers on the train to New York as the airfield (Idlewilde in those days) was closed. There were no flight or duty time limitations in those days; we just carried on until we and our passengers had reached the final destination.

David Beaty operating as Captain on one of my flights

During my two years of flying – I did one trip to Sydney, one to Santiago, Chile via Panama and the others were all transatlantic to New York or Montreal, or to the Caribbean, Nassau and Jamaica via the Azores and Bermuda. Usually these were on a Constellation but the Monarch service which started in March '51 to New York was a superior flight. This was by Stratocruiser (which first flew the Atlantic in December 1949) where you went 'downstairs' to the bar/lounge, and all the seats converted into bunk beds – curtained off with properly made up beds. Can you imagine the work involved?! After preparing and serving a silver service dinner and clearing up, you then had to convert the seats into bunks, make up the beds and eventually (after a short break) wake everyone with breakfast in bed – then return the bunks to seats! A young Elizabeth Taylor, at the very start of her career having starred in 'Black Velvet' and already married to Conrad Hilton's son, was one of the many stars to whom I remember taking breakfast.

Twice, in New York, I experienced an extra-curricular activity. The first time I was asked to make an announcement over the tannoy system at the airport as they wanted an "English" voice. Secondly they were filming a movie called Miss Pilgrims Progress and I had to stand at the top of the steps greeting passengers.

My kaleidoscopic memories of two years of flying are many and varied; from exhaustion and apprehension to glamour and 'unbelievability'! To be enjoying tropical Caribbean beaches in the post war period when everything at home was still rationed and foreign travel for holidays was unheard of for the average person; it was only for the wealthy and the nobility.

Most stops along our routes were known for a 'shopping must'! Lisbon was noted for its colourful baskets – we all arrived home with several (although they were quite cumbersome) but they had a ready market! New York, of course, was nylons and chocolate, Lima was llama wool slippers. And on all our trips our duty free ration of cigarettes and booze was soon snapped up!

My one trip to Australia was memorable and lasted about 3 weeks, which allowed for 3 crew 'slips' on the outward and return journey. The route was operated by the Constellation – all first class seats – around 33/34 passengers with one chief steward, one steward, one stewardess and all meals cooked on board and served 'silver service'! On all routes, before each flight left we were given a passenger list, which included specifically identified VIP's and any other relevant information. Any passenger travelling the route uninterrupted would have taken about 2½ days with refuelling stops along the way. Fortunately the seats reclined and most passengers were able to sleep. There were usually about 6 stops – typically Tripoli, Lydda, Karachi, Calcutta, Singapore, Jakarta, before we reached Darwin and Sydney.

One of the favourite stopovers for the crew was Singapore. Here we stayed at the Sea View Hotel, a seaside position with a circular dance floor with all the same echoing effects as the dome at St Paul's Cathedral. Amazingly you could hear what people were saying the other side of the ballroom! Nearby was the swimming club where we spent many happy hours and just outside the gate of the hotel was Mooi Heng's where we would meet for drinks.

Mooi Heng's, Singapore

On my return trip somehow I managed to contact my cousin Leo who was an army engineering officer stationed there and we met for a drink on the terrace of the Raffles Hotel.

My scariest flight was between Darwin and Sydney. It was night time so the cabin lights were turned low and the passengers all strapped in trying to sleep through an almighty storm. The aircraft was thrown around the sky with thunder and lightning all around and every few minutes we would 'free fall' some feet so we were thrown around and had to cling on to whatever we could. It was really frightening – but we all survived – and we finally arrived in Sydney. The crew were put into a guest house at the north end of Bondi Beach where my random memories are of having lamb chops for breakfast and getting badly sunburnt for the first and last time in my life on the famous beach. I walked across 'The Bridge' – but there was no sign of an opera house in 1950.

Initially my most frequent flights across the Atlantic were to New York or Montreal and then they were to the Caribbean, usually stopping at the Azores and Bermuda. Bermuda became one of my favourite stops down the routes where we often spent a few days at the St George Hotel, now a club, but then a luxurious hotel. There was an elegant lounge with a resident American female pianist playing the latest American songs. Amongst the most memorable was the score from South Pacific which hadn't yet reached London and she serenaded one of our Captains with 'Some Enchanted Evening' across a crowded room! We walked or took a horse drawn buggy down to the small beach and nearby historical landmarks.

At St David's Lighthouse, Bermuda.

With Jean in a horse drawn buggy, Bermuda

Panama City was an interesting stop and two of us made the train journey alongside the canal from Panama to Colon. The canal was first initiated by

Ferdinand de Lessops of Suez Canal fame, but the construction was taken over by the Americans. It is approx. 50 miles long and took about 30 years to build, eventually opening in 1914. However it came at a heavy cost with many of the workers losing their lives to malaria and yellow fever. The train terminus for Panama City is at Balboa on the Pacific side of the isthmus. The train then follows the route of the canal on the Eastern side travelling north to Colon on the Atlantic coast. The track went under a tunnel and passed the narrow Miraflores and Pedro Miguel locks. Looking out of the left hand window on the train it was an amazing sight to see the large liners dwarfing the adjacent land.

Flying south from Panama we stopped at Lima – capital of Peru – known on the route for 'pisco sours' and llama slippers!! We were then on our way to Santiago and after landing we had a long drive to a guest house at the foot of the Andes.

Our stops in Jamaica were at the capital, Kingston, on the south-west coast, which although a rough area was nothing like the dangerous city of today. We stayed either at the Myrtle Beach Hotel or the Mona Guest House. The former was in town near the harbour and the latter at the foothills of the Blue Mountains. The airport in Kingston is the Pallisadoes airport at the end of the peninsular. At one time we were the first aircraft to land after a hurricane – there were boats lying around the airfield in various states – having been blown ashore and there were also wrecked small aircraft amongst the debris. I also experienced the 'shaking' of an earthquake while staying in Kingston.

Our other Caribbean destination was Nassau, Bahamas. After meeting Peter in Cairo, catching up with him in Luxor and between postings in London, he was posted to Nassau. I went to stay for a week's holiday in July '51. He had a little house with a small narrow garden leading on to the seafront by the harbour. The view ahead was of Hog Island, now more grandly called Paradise Island, and there was no large bridge connecting it to the mainland – just a little ferry. The beach was nearly always deserted except for a few locals. It was idyllic – clean, clear sea with sting rays basking in the shallow water and one small hut providing cold drinks.

With Peter in Nassau 1951

On the beach in Nassau looking for shells

On the harbour quays local fishermen cooked their freshly caught crayfish and lobsters in an oilcan of boiling water. In Bay Street, the exclusive shops sold duty free goods including Lalique glassware and expensive perfumes alongside the local souvenirs of basketware, shells and tortoiseshell. The library in an old building behind the government offices had a spiral staircase and nooks and crannies with chairs to sit and read. There were restaurants serving good meals – a nightclub called The Spider's Web on the harbour wall with sharks swimming outside – romantic at night – but really grotty by day!

In November of 1951 Peter came home on leave and we went to Paris for a romantic and touristy weekend! We travelled on a boat on the Seine and walked along its banks; 'did' the Eiffel Tower, Montmartre, Notre Dame and numerous cafes and the Musee d'Orsay. How did we fit it all in?! We came back engaged and decided to get married straight away. So in a hectic 10 days I resigned, we arranged a small wedding and on 17 November on a blustery, wet day we got married. Clothes rationing was still in force, so no wedding dresses were available!

Our Wedding photograph November 1951

After a few days 'honeymoon' in Brighton, Peter had to return to Nassau and I followed a week later. The bachelor house provided was a square box on the water's edge! We adopted a stray kitten and between Peter's shifts we explored the island.

Our 'box' by the sea Nassau Dec 1951

Our 'box' by the sea Nassau Dec 1951

With our stray cat.

PART TWO

Chapter 7

Bahamas and Jamaica (1952-1955)

It was December 1951 and for the next nearly 25 years I was an 'expat's wife' and all that that entailed!

There are a string of adjectives and words to describe those years, but monotonous and boring are not amongst them! I had fantastic opportunities to travel and to 'live' in several countries as opposed to just 'visiting' them. I also experienced many interesting and unusual situations and events. It was an exciting, fascinating, frustrating and nomadic lifestyle. Experiencing cancellations, uncertainties, adjustments, separations and responsibilities, last minute alterations – new friends, locations and occupations, last minute changes, disappointments and happy surprises, shortages and luxuries. Packing and unpacking and adapting, first on my own and then with one and then two daughters, with UK homes and schools to manage I became very familiar with airports, driving to and from them, arriving on time, wasting time, finding parking and supporting Duty Free shops!!

But to get back to Nassau! Nassau is the capital of the Bahamas. There was one main street, Bay Street lined on one side by luxurious tourist shops and on the opposite by the harbour with a flourishing straw market and other waterside activities. Mail boats would ply across the shallow Bahamian Banks and provide a vital life line to the many outlying islands. Their cargoes of the full range of household goods from tinned meat to toilet rolls and livestock to wood and nails would be piled up on the decks while passengers would hope for some soft packaging which might provide a comfy place to settle for the passage. Meanwhile the earlier and smaller cruise ships would dock in the centre of town for a few hours, and even in those days, dwarfed the little town. There was, and still is, a lot of wealth in a small area. There were luxurious beach front hotels which, in the days before package holidays, only opened for the winter season. The Duke of Windsor was one time Governor of the Bahamian Islands and Government

House was a fine colonial building with flamingos in the garden where the Governor entertained expats on the Queen's official birthday in June.

Nassau is situated on the island of New Providence surrounded by several large low, lying and sparsely populated islands as well as many small cays, well over 600 in all. The surrounding sea is shallow and sheltered. Its clarity is amazing, revealing corals, tropical fish and shells, sea-fans and sponges. I started to build up a large collection of shells and became an amateur conchologist! Over time my collection was added to and accompanied us around the world in tea chests.

We soon moved from our 'box' by the sea to a newly built bungalow further inland. This was a great improvement, but was isolated and there was no phone! But I did luckily learn to drive and passed my test thanks to Peter giving me lessons on the old airfield.

Georgie Cottage, Soldier Road

The day it was announced that George V1 had died we had arranged our house warming party. There were several families and bachelors working for UK based companies and we had soon become part of this community. We felt a bit guilty going ahead as there was an air of sadness about, especially as the Bahamas was a very loyal colony, but with no phone there was no way we could contact everyone to cancel it – and I hadn't heard the news until mid-morning. So we went ahead; I had made about 400 canapes and snacks and the party was a lively affair ... with local rum of course being the preferred drink.

Soon after, we moved again as it was not practical, work wise, for Peter not to be contactable by phone when emergencies arose at the airport; no mobiles in those days! This time it was to an old wooden bungalow on the East coast road and near the end of the developed area. There was a road between the bungalow and the sea, where we had a small beach and before long a boat and a fish pot. The boat was small and with an outboard motor that never worked. So we rowed out to the fish pot where we caught some strange fish, none of them edible! Then one night during hurricane force winds our little boat was smashed against the rocks and was a right-off.

With Peter and our boat

The bungalow, being built of wood, was full of termites with little piles of dust appearing where the insects had been busy. The property was called Twynham Cottage and was owned by the three Twynham sisters who had inherited a large area of land originally purchased by their father, sight unseen, in an auction in London some time previously for about £150!

We came home for Peter to do a course and later for some leave. We were lucky compared to many people working for other companies abroad as we did have annual leave; some people had longer contracts of two/three years with no home leave.

In the summer, between our visits home, I learnt that I was expecting our first baby. We were so happy, but unfortunately I didn't have a very good pregnancy and felt ill most of the time. Peter did a wonderful job of cooking and looking after me. Although due on February 22 1953 she was not actually born until April 16 and was still born. Everyone was so kind and looked after me very well. After a few days in hospital I returned and rested at home. Peter had found an hotel in Miami called Hotel Patricia so we went over and stayed for 2 or 3 days and later came back to England for some leave.

On returning in July, I got myself a job with a local lumber company called The Maura Lumber Co.. They had a large shop selling builders' hardware and kitchen equipment. I soon settled in and was able to do the ordering from 'Prestige' and other well-known companies and at Christmas we stocked a selection of toys. I had only been working there for 5 months when just before Christmas we were posted to Montego Bay. Settling down and then getting moved on was to become the story of my life!

In December 1953, two years after arriving in Nassau, we were making our home in Montego Bay on the North coast of Jamaica. As our house was not ready for us we stayed at a guest house called Hacton House. We had an en-suite and a veranda overlooking the bay and luxuriant pot plants filled the room and veranda. Our next door neighbour at the guest house was Charlie Smirk the 1952 Derby winner.

In spite of the luxurious hotels along the coast, the town of Montego Bay itself was quite dirty and smelly and small. It had open drains and gulleys and after a heavy downpour the main road was blocked by thick mud, stones, branches and rubbish washed down from the hillside. And yes the rain was heavy. It is surprising that although the West Indian islands are known to have luxuriant vegetation and tropical growth, many people do not associate the idea of bad weather with these islands in the sun! The weather can be very nasty, especially in the hurricane season which extends roughly from July to November. Then the skies can be dark with rain, the seas can be wild and the wind can flatten whole areas of banana plantations overnight. A tropical island in bad weather can be a really miserable place. The houses are built for the sun and are usually very open and chilly when the temperature drops, the roads have no proper drainage and they soon are flooded, there is no indoor entertainment or amusement for visitors and tourists and worst of all the rain brings out the mosquitoes. How those horrible little biting insects can ruin an evening!

Montego Bay in those days was better known as a winter holiday resort for the wealthy Americans and the probably even wealthier British who could afford to keep a house there or stay at one of the luxury hotels. Because of the inclement weather during the summer months the 'season' ended at Easter and everything closed down for the summer! Further to the east of Montego Bay were scattered the winter homes of the rich and famous including: – the debonair Noel Coward, the master of espionage Ian Fleming and swash-buckling Errol Flynn.

Errol Flynn bought property on the North coast in the 1940's and was well known for his lavish parties and rafting on the Rio Grande. Its source was in the mountains and then its course ran steeply through the bamboos to the coast. He died in 1959 and is reputed to have been buried with 6 bottles of whiskey in his coffin!

In 1946 Ian Fleming also bought a property nearby, which he called Golden Eye. He made use of his military experience and wrote his many books on the exploits of James Bond, the action hero. In searching for a name for his hero – he wanted something simple – he searched his library and came across a book written earlier on Birds of The West Indies by a James Bond. He had found the name he wanted. He wrote all 13 James Bond novels whilst in Jamaica. Ian Fleming, like Errol Flynn, died at a very young age.
Meanwhile Noel Coward, a contemporary and friend of both Flynn and Fleming, also bought a property in Jamaica and had his retreat of 'Blue Harbour' built in 1948 where he entertained lavishly. Later, looking for a more peaceful residence, he had another 'retreat' built, which he called Firefly, where he painted and wrote in the beautiful and picturesque surroundings. Firefly is now operated as a museum.

It was part of Peter's job as manager of the local airport to meet and greet and facilitate the passage of the rich and famous – so he met a range of personalities including those mentioned above and their many guests, especially during the popular winter months. On one occasion a very distinguished and very wealthy large lady (who carried all before her!) took a shine to him and invited us to dinner at her grand house. There was a very long dining table and many staff to serve her guests. She sat at one end with Peter on her right and her small hen pecked husband at the far end of the table. I was seated at a small 'overflow' table to the side! I think I enjoyed my meal more.

In February we moved into our house. Peter was ill with bronchitis so it was a blessing that I could drive the car that we had inherited from a previous staff member, or we would have been stranded. It was an upside down house with the garage and maids quarters below. We had a real 'coal black' maid called Ada and also a young garden boy. A very handsome and superior Siamese cat completed the household! Ada would do the washing, the cleaning and some cooking. She would often buy a scraggy chicken and keep it for days in the yard tied up with a piece of string, fattening it up, before putting it in the stew pot.

Our house in Montego Bay

Ada, our maid

Soon after moving in, Francis, Peter's cousin and a Captain with the Royal Mail Line arrived in Kingston for a few days. Kingston, the capital, and on the south east coast was a 4½hours drive away over the mountains. We set off early one evening to join him for a drink on board. The drive was up and down mountains and badly maintained roads; it was dark and a very hairy drive! Seeing a pair of headlights approaching you took care, as often the darkness concealed a heavily laden lorry of sacks of sugar extending several feet beyond the lights on either side! This did not make for a relaxing journey. Eventually we arrived, saw Francis for a few hours, stayed overnight in an hotel and then returned the next day in daylight!

With Peter and Francis [Peter's cousin]

Although Jamaica had its advantages, we did long to see snowdrops, daffodils and Brussel sprouts during the winter months! Filling in time was quite a challenge. There was a local beach club called Doctors Cave where we would regularly go swimming in the clear, blue sea. Everyone went there on Sundays ... it was beach, beer and then back home for a siesta! But you can't spend all your time on the beach so I acquired an ancient Singer sewing machine and started some dressmaking; I also started assembling and making simple costume jewellery but then, before I got really organised, we were moved on again.

We came home in July for leave and by this time I was 'expecting' again and I planned to stay in England with Peter's family until the baby was born. Sue was born the following January at Queen Charlotte's Hospital where Peter's mother worked as a ward sister. Conditions for visitors were very different in those days – visiting hours were strictly 6-6.30pm. When Peter visited on the 4th January he was told that 'nothing would happen' until the following morning and to ring at 8 am. Sue was actually born at 23.45 that night so it was about 8 hrs before Peter knew that he was the father of a baby girl and he didn't see her until 'visiting' that evening. Sue weighed 7lbs 11½oz which was quite significant as will be seen later! After the birth and the normal stay of two weeks in hospital I went to a convalescent home in Hastings for two weeks which was run by Queen Charlotte's. In the meantime, after a year in Montego Bay Peter had been posted to Tripoli in Libya, North Africa.

Majorie, Peter's mother, in her nurse's uniform

Chapter 8

Libya and Ceylon (1955 – 1957)

At 4 weeks old Sue was in a carry cot, transferring to a sky-cot on board the flight to Tripoli where she started her nomadic life. Comfortable flying was still the norm; a sky-cot was attached to the luggage rack and she slept peacefully. There was a separate and spacious lady's loo equipped with a changing table and the usual supply of Elizabeth Arden products.

We arrived at Idris airport, named after the reigning monarch King Idris, who had led and reunited the country after the long Italian occupation which was finally ended during the Second World War. There was still however a strong Italian culture with many Italians still living there. We stayed at the Del Mahari Hotel until other accommodation was found for us. The hotel was on the coast road and a passage under the main road took guests to the promenade and harbour opposite. My long-lasting memory of the dining room at the hotel was the magnificent silver cheese dish with a swing dome containing a whole gorgonzola which was always served after dinner and at its creamiest best.

Postcard of the Del Mahari Hotel

We soon moved into our flat. It was on the top floor of a block occupied by Italian families – with one other English couple on the ground floor, an army major and his wife. Conditions were fairly primitive. The kitchen had a primus stove and 'makeshift' oven of a biscuit tin – and after dark, when you switched the light on there was the scurry of cockroaches disappearing under the cupboards and the smallest grain of sugar would attract a trail of ants. In the bathroom the method of heating water for the bath was a wood fire which you had to light under a geyser filled with water. This was Sue's first home! Peter was working a lot of night shifts at the airport as that was when the majority of aircraft came and went. So I had to find my way around and lug a pram up and down stairs. Most of the locals spoke a mixture of Arabic and Italian – so shopping was fun! It was a long time before I realised that the fish I was buying was shark! But it tasted good – a solid meaty fish.

At the fish shop

With Sue

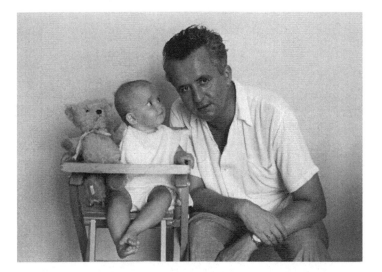

Peter with Sue

Our household possessions arrived by 'freight' a few days after we moved to the flat. These were contained in carefully packed tea-chests, but however carefully packed the contents could not withstand unexpected treatment. The sound of puffing and panting of an elderly Arab arriving outside the door of our top floor flat and the inevitable crash when the chest slipped from his back to the concrete landing had the expected effect! Most of all our precious china was broken.

My mother came to visit us for a short holiday. At that time she was working for Freddie Laker who was running Aviation Traders. She came to Malta from London as 'supernummary crew' which was quite something at that time! She flew on from Malta on a BOAC flight. Ken (Peter's cousin), who was working for Barclays overseas, was also in Tripoli for a short spell during our stay there.

With my mother in old Tripoli

Ken with Sue

Members of the British armed forces were stationed here and fortunately we were able to use their facilities. One evening we went to a beach barbeque organised by the army. I was wearing a very distinctive cotton dress with a large floral design, when lo and behold a lady wearing an identical dress approached me. I had bought mine in a shop in Miami and she had bought hers in New York and we'd both ended up in North Africa! Small world!

With Peter at a BBQ

The weather ranged from hot and sunny to stormy. One night the hailstones were so big they broke the bedroom window! Later during our stay I woke one morning and heard dripping water. I went into Sue's room to discover that it was flooded. The ceiling was bowed down with the weight of water – luckily the cot was not directly underneath, but it was beginning to float! Peter, of course, was at the airport, so I dashed down to the ground floor flat and luckily Major Eden was in. He went up on the flat roof where the water tank was situated and discovered that the ball-cock was missing and hence the constant overflow and subsequent flooding. This apparently was quite a common event as the entrance and stairwell were open and small boys would steal the ball-cocks and sell them!

On our return from Tripoli late in 1955, we rented a house on the coastal road at Greatstone-on Sea. It was very bleak in December as most of the houses were shut for the winter. Turning right out of the front door was Dungeness power station and left to New Romney and beyond. Straight ahead was a very rough sea! There was no phone and Peter was in London. Sue was 11months old and had decided that digestive biscuits were to be her diet and that she was 'a strongman' as she would lug around a portable typewriter! At this time we had a big 'hiccup' and decided that we wanted to settle in England. We found a four storey house with 18 bedrooms in Margate and decided to run a hotel!! Whilst we negotiated, Sue and I moved to the Nayland Rock Hotel in Margate while Peter was in London doing a course. Luckily he hadn't taken the step of resigning – but we did complete on the house and then started having cold feet. We had had an elementary survey done (which was not very helpful as the solicitor, surveyor and the agent were all in league!) but soon discovered that although there were wash basins in all the rooms there was no water supply above the second floor. We also found other problems and as a result Peter went to the mortgage company, told them that he had been posted to Calcutta and wouldn't be able to make any repayments! Heaven knows how or why, but they did let him cancel the agreement and we were free and had learnt our lesson.

Although the story about Calcutta was a total fabrication, by the middle of the year we were in Ceylon! This was a typical 'temporary' posting to relieve someone who was sick. My letters back to my mother, however, detail the many changes of plans during this particular posting, with frequent requests for hotels in London to be booked (as we had no home back in the UK), cots and high-chairs to be arranged etc. only then to be cancelled days later. It was a disruptive six months although we did enjoy being there so always made the most of the extensions to our stay. It did however mean that we had to change our place of abode several times staying at two different hotels, two flats and a house! The lack of routine played havoc with Sue's potty training!

One of the flats was at Turret Road, No. 191, which I have since discovered was the base for the RAF Broadcasting Station during the war. Known as SEAC (South East Asian Company) it was the predecessor of what became Air Ceylon.

191 Turret Road, one of the flats we stayed in

While Peter worked long shifts at the airport, Sue and I adjusted to our various forms of accommodation and amused ourselves at home. Sue was at the age when she was able to get into everything and was curious and full of energy so most of my time was spent just keeping track of her! We joined a swimming club, as the sea at the coast was rough with strong undercurrents, and would often go there in the afternoons. It was a good opportunity for Sue to play with other children and to burn off some energy by splashing around in the pool. Getting around however was expensive as we had to take taxis everywhere. Occasionally I was able to leave Sue with a nanny for a few hours so that I could shop by myself.

Known as the Pearl of the East because of its shape, Ceylon (now known as Sri Lanka) lies only 18 miles from the South Eastern tip of India and only a few miles north of the Equator. Nature has endowed the island with an abundance of natural riches, low lying coastal strips supporting coconut, pineapple and banana groves, the cool, hilly uplands of the tea plantations and, in-between, paddy fields of rice and large rubber plantations. We were able to see much of this diverse range of vegetation on our first 'outing' en route to Ratnapura, about 50 miles inland from Colombo, which was a centre for gem mining. There were teams of locals 'mining' for the local gem stones in a very primitive and dangerous way, using rickety bamboo scaffolding at the entrances to the mines which all looked very precarious. We were also able to see the stones being cut and polished by hand. This was fascinating and combined with the interesting diversions en route of seeing rubber plantations, brick making and watching the farmers planting rice in the paddy fields; it made a fabulous day.

On the way to the gem pit

The bamboo scaffolding at the gem pit

One of the workers at the gem pit

One of the many jewellery stores

Outside the Ratnapura Rest House with Sue

With Peter working long shifts and with the expense of having to hire a car and driver for our excursions we only managed 3 days out during our six month posting. Our second was not quite as successful as our first. We decided to go to Kandy, but unfortunately our day was curtailed by the fact that Peter had a chest infection and Sue became car sick. Then the camera jammed! However we were able to visit the famous lake and the Temple of the Tooth. The relic of the tooth (allegedly having belonged to Buddha) was kept in a two-story inner shrine fronted by two large elephant tusks. The relic rested on a solid gold lotus flower, encased in jewelled caskets that sat on a throne. In front of the temple was a pretty lake and whilst we were there, there was a procession of highly decorated elephants which were considered to be sacred to Buddha.

It was interesting to get a feel for some of the history of the island and its people. Equally we followed the politics of the day. There were two main ethnic groups, the Tamils and the Sinhalese, the latter being the more numerous and powerful. Both had their own language but during 1956 the Sinhalese introduced a 'Sinhala Only Act' replacing English as the official language. This failed to give any recognition to the Tamil language. Although both languages are now formally recognized, at the time it caused massive conflict between the two groups, resulting in large numbers of Tamils being forced out of their jobs as they were unable to converse in Sinhala. The country was also going through 'post-Independence' adaptations with the RAF bases closing in 1956 causing mainly Tamil job losses. Many of the British tea planters were also choosing to return to the UK which did provide opportunities for some Ceylonese to take over the management of the estates. The local papers were full of the latest tales of strife and upheaval. Whilst we were able keep in touch with local news, news of home and international news was more difficult to obtain. Unfortunately most of the English newspapers on board the incoming aircraft had already been taken off , but we were able to hear the BBC World Service News twice a day at 7.30am and 6.30pm. The Suez crisis took the main headlines and had a direct impact in Colombo. Several British cruise passengers from the Orient Line were stranded when the liners stopped calling into Ceylon, choosing to avoid the Suez Canal and go via Cape Town instead. The planes consequently filled up with the extra passengers.

Whilst my letters home to my mother showed a great interest in the Suez Crisis, my main interest was looking after Sue! Whilst her development seemed to be slow she certainly experienced a great deal at a very young age and maybe that was her way of coping with all the change and variety. She got used to seeing elephants walk along the streets; feeding the monkeys in the zoo and watching the oxen pull their heavy loads. One day when we were staying at The Mount Lavinia Hotel a snake charmer came to perform to the guests on the hotel terrace. Sue was very intrigued but then amazed when she saw her Daddy wrap the snake around his neck!

View of the coastal railway from The Mount Lavinia Hotel

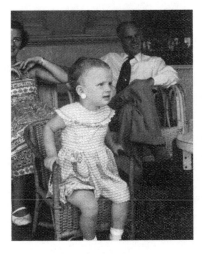

Sue's reaction!

Peter on the terrace of The Mount Lavinia Hotel with a snake around his neck

Our final excursion out of Colombo was to Galle. It was a hot but beautiful day and we drove along the bamboo and coconut lined coastal roads of the west coast. We stopped at Hikkaduwa, which at the time, was a small fishing village; a beautiful spot with a reef. It was in this year (1956) that the science fiction writer Arthur C. Clarke opened up his scuba diving centre there and it was his home until his death in 2008. Galle has a harbour and an old Portuguese fort, later used by the Dutch.

The coastal road to Galle lined with tall coconut palms

Bullock carts in the streets

After six enjoyable months we were sad to return to the UK in the middle of November, but anxious to find out to where we would be posted next.

By Christmas 1956 we had moved on and were in Istanbul for a few weeks staying in a large hotel in a room facing the Bosphorus. Our room had a veranda overlooking the water, which was always very busy. We went on a ferry for a day trip up the Bosphorus – very cheap and very lively with music and singing. We had a visit to the bazaar, the largest undercover market in the world (so we were told!); about 3,000 stalls! Peter bought me a little bracelet with hand painted panels. (Unfortunately, along with all my collection of world-wide jewellery, it was stolen some years later.)

Chapter 9

Bahrain (1957-1962)

By April 1957 we were in Bahrain for a 'permanent' posting of 5 years! What a change from our nomadic life of one temporary posting after another. Now we could 'settle' for a few years.

Peter had gone ahead and Sue and I followed travelling First Class! I think it worth quoting from a letter I wrote to my mother at the time describing the journey.

"We had a very good journey out, it did not seem nearly so tiring as usual. The weather was beautiful all the way and Sue was very good. We left for Rome at 10.30. At pre-lunch cocktails Sue really fancied herself with a sherry glass of tomato juice and a canapé! We had an excellent champagne lunch followed by coffee and liquers, during which we could look down on the snow covered peaks of the Alps bathed in sunlight. Mont Blanc was pointed out just below us.

Our stay in Rome was short, about an hour, during which we had tea or a cool drink. On the way from Rome to Istanbul Sue had a sleep and dinner was served, again a very good meal complete with cocktails, champagne and liquers. At Istanbul we had to wait nearly two hours as we were ahead of schedule and Kuwait, our next stop had no facilities for night landings. Sue passed the time 'on the run' with a fellow passenger, aged 3, also called Sue!

Between Istanbul and Kuwait, a flight of just under six hours, we all dozed and then had breakfast before we landed. Kuwait from the air was a small gathering of beige coloured buildings set in an expanse of sand, a truly depressing sight unrelieved by any splash of colour. The airport building is simple, sandy and sordid. This being the month of Ramadan the Mohamedans fast from sunrise to sunset; they take no liquid, no food and no tobacco. These restrictions are passed on to transit passengers!

It was only an hours flight to Bahrain, the sun was bright and the sea very clear. The water is varying shades of green being transparent in the shallow waters near the coast. Occasionally the sandy wastes are broken by small groups of buildings and a jetty out of all proportion stretching like a thin searching finger its tip reaching the deeper water. A few ships can be seen steaming to and fro, their arrow like wake more easily visible than the ships themselves.

I felt great relief at the sight of Bahrain; at least here was some greenery in the form of date palms!. The airport is on a small island connected to Bahrain (which is the largest island in the group, which is known by that name) by a causeway.

Manama is the capital town, in the north eastern tip of the island and is where we are staying. The Rest House is run by B.O.A.C. and is of a very high standard. There is only one other hotel which does not compare and which does not hold an alcohol licence. Oil tanker crews and aircrews, amongst others, all use the Rest House. We have two rooms here until our bungalow is ready; one large bedroom and a larger still sitting room where Sue can run wild! We went to see our bungalow today. It will be ready in about six weeks. There are two being built together and the other will also be occupied by a B.O.A.C. family, so we won't be too cut off."

Bahrain is an island in the Persian Gulf off the east coast of Saudi Arabia.

Bahrain in the late 1950's was a country of contrasts. The discovery of oil in the early 30's had brought some modernisation but equally the country was seeped in its traditional Arab ways. Local fishing vessels called dhows were based in the harbours and still sailed between the islands. Prior to the introduction of cultured pearls from Japan they were used by the pearl fishers, when pearling had been a flourishing and significant industry. As well as its Arab heritage there were also some signs of the occupation by the Portuguese in the 1500's and the ruins of one of their forts still stand.

We soon moved to our bungalow near the Sheik's Palace, which was only used for visiting Heads of State or similar. It was after a short time that we discovered there were no locals available to help in the house or with Sue but that a nursery at the convent school was available. We tried it out just for two hours in the morning and she loved it and went off happily at 2 years 3 months with her little bag with a Ribena drink and a sandwich in a cigarette tin! This enabled me to shop in the hot, dusty town on my own.

Sue getting off the bus after her first day at school

Peter was working at the airport on Muharrak Island. The airport was a busy one being one of the most advanced airports in the Gulf region and therefore used extensively as a re-fuelling stop by the many airlines plying between Europe and Asia and Australia. It was an important base for BOAC with the development from flying boats to the first jet planes during the 50's. It was also the home to the Gulf Aviation Company, formed by an ex RAF pilot Freddie Bosworth in the 40's providing a network within the Gulf region. On Freddie's sad and premature death in a flying accident in 1951 BOAC took a large shareholding in the airline, then called Gulf Air. (Nevil Shute's novel 'Round The Bend' was largely drawn from Freddie's life story.)

In addition to the team of Brits who worked for BOAC, both at the airport and at the town office, there were quite a lot of other expats around – working for the oil company, BAPCO (British American Petroleum Company), the tobacco company BAT (British American Tobacco), Cable and Wireless with various agents and reps for other companies. The Navy also had a base at Jufair.

The climate was not so good especially in the summer with temperatures reaching well over a very humid 100 degrees. It was a '3 shirts a day and a hand towel around the neck' kind of weather. We only had air-conditioning in the bedrooms – and one evening a week electricity was cut off due to shortages. The houses had flat roofs so we migrated there with drinks on those evenings. Most of the children suffered from prickly heat – including Sue. However in Jan/Feb the temperature could fall to about 65 degrees and we were freezing with no heating and stone floors!

After a few months I was offered a part-time job at the hospital. I was to be secretary to the Chief Surgeon (an ex-Harley Street man). So armed with a medical dictionary and my two typing fingers I tackled medical reports and coped with phone calls! This was where I became familiar with the word 'carcinoma'. So many locals seemed to have large growths on their neck and faces. The surgeon had a 'Pernod-drinking' eccentric wife, who kept ringing up and didn't seem to understand that he couldn't just leave the theatre mid-op to speak to her. One morning she was very insistent and couldn't wait to tell him that she had decided that her budgie needed a mate!

As there were no local maids available, many expats employed girls brought in from the Seychelles. This was quite a commitment as we were responsible for them and their welfare. It was also quite a jump into the unknown on their behalf too, as the journey by sea took about two weeks and they had limited knowledge of the family they were about to live with. Anyway we went ahead and Odette arrived in November 1957. The boat anchored about 4 miles offshore due to the shallow waters and we went out to meet her in a launch. First impressions were good and luckily Sue took to her at once. She only spoke French! And that was the Seychellois version! We soon managed and she was able to cook, wash, iron and look after Sue. She also had a friend working in a house nearby which was a great help. It was quite a thing having four to feed on the limited supplies available. We had a lot of fish, which were usually about 6lbs in weight which Odette filleted and skinned. The food shops didn't have freezers so shopping was difficult – no fresh milk nor veg – everything was tinned including, to our amazement, whole cauliflowers.

I played a lot of Scrabble and we bought a set in January 1958 which Sue, Liz and I still use today. It has nice wooden 'tiles' instead of the modern plastic ones and we still use the bag for the tiles that my mother made from some left over curtain material from the bungalow! My cousin Leo was also in Bahrain about this time and enjoyed the odd game of Scrabble with us.

We were home on leave for a couple of months and returned in the April; it was very hot and humid on our return. We moved to a compound of 5 'walled-in' bungalows with an armed guard, near the Gymkhana Club and on the edge of the disused racecourse. The temperature had been over 100 degrees for several months so it was good to be near the swimming pool at the club but it was still an effort to walk the short distance.

By July I was expecting again and feeling low, but better after the doctor prescribed 12 salt tablets a day! One really does need extra salt in hot, humid weather. I went home again during July for a while although going back and forth to England was always a problem as we had no home 'base' and had to stay in hotels or stay with family or friends.

On my return it was still hot and sticky although we did try and do 'something' most evenings as it was too hot to stay at home and do nothing, but on the other hand it was too hot to enjoy doing anything! Entertaining was a nightmare hot dishes soon got cold under the fan and jellies melted within minutes in the heat!

I was home again by mid-December and 7 months pregnant! The only accommodation I could find for the short period until I was due in hospital was a bed-sit on the second floor of a house over-looking Clapham Common. It was cold and I had to carry buckets of coal upstairs for the coal fire which was the only form of heating. There was no bathroom so I had to give Sue a bath in a bowl in front of the fire. Going shopping for food was a nightmare on the bus with an active and very voluble Sue talking to everyone while I was carrying a heavy bag of food! Eventually I made it to Barts Hospital (again with the influence of my mother-in-law who had trained there in the days when nurses had to pay to be trained!) Peter came home and again strict visiting times were in force 6-6.30pm. So he was sent away at 6.30 and Liz was born at 6.45! She weighed exactly 7lbs 11½oz, the same as Sue! I had by this time got bronchial pneumonia and was constantly coughing. Liz was christened Elizabeth Jane, although we had wanted to call her Jane as her first name until we realised that that would have given her the unfortunate combination of initials J.E.L. and we could foresee a nightmare stage at school when she would have been called Jelly!! So the first few months she was called Jane, but it soon became Elizabeth and not until much later was it Liz or Lizzy.

I transgress. After 2 weeks in hospital and another 2 weeks in St Leonards convalescent home, Liz too travelled abroad in a sky cot at 4 weeks old, as the three of us went back to Bahrain.

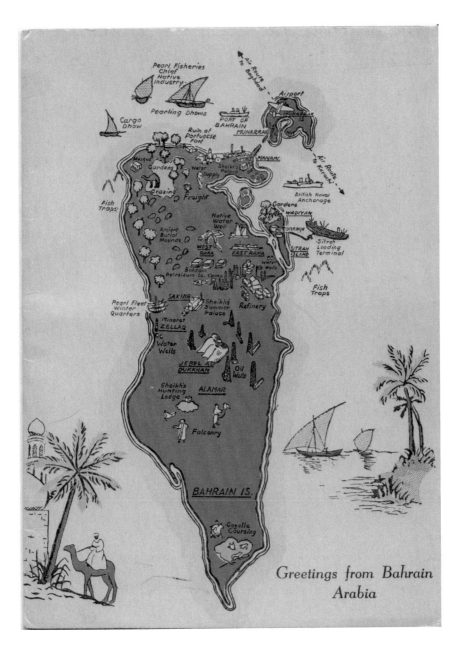

Map of Bahrain [taken from a 1951 Raphael Tuck Christmas card]

At the entrance to the Taj Mahal

Peter in front of the Taj Mahal

Looking back from the Taj Mahal towards the entrance

The Qutub Minar, Delhi

Liz at Delhi Zoo

With Sue and Liz in their new school uniforms, with the car packed ready to go, outside Romney Cottage

Hindhead Court,
The Grove; the girls'
boarding house

Our house in Montego Bay

Peter with the girls at
Dunns River Falls,
Jamaica

Chapter 10

Bahrain (1957-1962)

At this time we were also negotiating to buy a flat. (Not so easy as everything had to be done via airmail letters as there were no emails or even phone calls!) It was on the top floor of a new block of flats opposite Virginia Water station. In June we eventually heard that everything was settled – mortgage arranged etc. solicitors and vendors happy and I arranged to come home at the end of July with the girls. Peter was still very busy with only two staff covering the 24hrs at the airport all the summer.

I seem to have spent July trying to furnish the flat with basics, by letter. We had various offers of furniture and bits and pieces from family members. I couldn't have done it without my mother's help as I seem to have written almost daily asking her to arrange everything from gas and electricity to looking at beds etc! Eventually I arrived home at the end of July with Sue (running everywhere) and Liz 5 months old. The priorities were a pram for Liz, 2 beds and bedding (no duvets in those days), a cot and all the other basics. In the end I stayed two nights in an hotel in Staines and gradually made the flat habitable for Peter who was coming home on leave in September.

We went back to Bahrain in November. Peter was busy with Comets and Boeing 707s passing through, Liz was crawling and a very happy baby and Sue was back at school very conscientiously learning the basics! We had been away a while and the house was full of sand and dust, so Odette and I had a big 'spring' cleaning job to do on our return including 13 pairs of curtains to wash! So it wasn't all fun and games overseas, although I did manage to play tennis, go swimming and go to parties! One notable one was organised by the oil company who, on Guy Fawkes night, laid on a great firework display from the end of a jetty with some on floating platforms with amazing reflections on the sea.

Christmas came and went and soon we were planning coming home again to our new flat. We also had to pay for Odette to go home for her leave – 2 weeks by boat via Bombay.

Liz with Odette [Detty]

1960 was another busy year with both Sue and Liz progressing well – Sue with school work and Liz with walking and eating a lot! Liz was very active and caused a near disaster one day. Peter was having a bath and had taken off his signet ring as it was a bit loose. Before we realised it Liz had gone into the bathroom, picked up his ring and dropped it down the loo! As the company owned several houses in Bahrain, it employed its own maintenance crew, so we duly called for a plumber, hoping that the ring had been caught in the U- bend or whatever. Unfortunately not, and the poor Bahraini workman nobly searched through the septic tank and miraculously he found it!

A new school was started by one of the wives and Sue was one of the first 6 to attend. It was called St Christopher's and is now a large and thriving school with over 2100 pupils from over 60 nations. With Sue at school and Liz being cared for by Odette, I took on the job of running the library at the Gymkhana club. They then created a post of 'Housekeeper' as so much food and drink – and therefore profits – were disappearing and so I combined the two which involved traditional library duties as well as overall control of the staff and organising parties. One of the first things I did was to introduce a card index system of the over 200 items of food and drink stock items and put a lock on the store room! Then the parties started with a Poppy Day dance for over 350 people which was a combined effort with the Army and Navy and two entertainment members on the committee. At Christmas we had a children's party for over 120 children.

Sue at the Gymkhana Club with her favourite rag doll

Sue was desperate to become a Brownie and was finally allowed to join the group even though she was technically 'under-age'. When she wasn't at Brownies or at the swimming club she was usually playing with her best friend, Susan. One day, Susan had found a box of matches and they began to play with them. They were playing on waste land and decided to set light to a small piece of dried palm leaf. Then they threw sand on top and it went out! However they then set fire to a larger pile but this time neither the sand, nor the egg cup of water that they brought from the kitchen, would put it out and the whole pile went up in flames. We returned home from shopping to be greeted by the fire brigade! Luckily no damage was done and the girls weren't hurt, but they were grounded for a few days and have never forgotten it!

I continued to be busy at the Gymkhana Club organising company do's and apparently turning the sheets from 'sides to middle' as one did in those days when they started showing signs of wear! In addition to organising parties at the Club, we also did quite a lot of home entertaining and I put on several 'fishy dos'. There was blue netting draped over the ceiling with red plastic fish 'swimming' around. I had fish shaped plates and dishes and the menu was fish orientated. All great fun!

One day Liz lost her teddy whilst out in the pram with Odette and was inconsolable so we searched the town for a replacement. We eventually found one which did the trick – it was much larger but it did pacify her.

In August there were 10 days of exceptionally hot and humid weather and there were several deaths. Our 'cold' water tank was on the top of the flat roof of our bungalow and I remember running a cold bath which was so hot we had to put ice cubes in to cool it down!

One day a friend and I had a rather hysterical morning. Seeing dead donkeys around was sadly not an unusual sight, but on this occasion, returning from shopping in town we passed one by the side of the road lying on its back with its legs straight up in the air; a grotesque sight so we felt that we had to do something about it. On our return home we started ringing around the different government departments trying to find one responsible for the removal of dead donkeys! Needless to say we didn't have much success although it did amuse us for a few hours!

Although Bahrain was developing quickly it was still very primitive in many ways as I was to discover one day. Some of the outlying villages were noted for making pottery so one morning a friend and I decided to visit one and see if we could buy a sample. We went off with a simple map to try and find the isolated village. It really was in the middle of nowhere and the locals were not used to seeing strange females drive in to find their kiln! They soon let us know that we were not welcome and started stoning the car, so as you can imagine we beat a hasty retreat.

In August we returned home for leave again and came back to Bahrain at the end of November. The following year 1962 our five year posting came to an end and we returned to our flat in Virginia Water in March.

To summarize our five year posting was really one of activity! We made several trips home over the years, I had two paid and one unpaid jobs, we had a new daughter and we bought a flat and had two tenants. The first was an RAF couple, he was a Wing Commander. They had many parties, upset the neighbours and there were cigarette burns in the carpet. The second was a Philippino and his wife. He was in the US Army and cook to the General. They were a delightful couple who got on with everyone and left the flat spotless!

Chapter 11

Romney Cottage and Brazil (1962 – 1965)

During our time in Bahrain both Peter and I suffered from various bouts of ill health and were glad to leave, but we had made many friends and I am still in touch with several families. On our return Peter went into the 'Pool', which consisted of staff available for short term and replacement postings often at short notice. So during the remainder of the year (1962) Peter went to Tripoli (again), Lisbon and San Francisco. He continued doing these temporary postings for the next 7 years until the girls were old enough to go to boarding school. I stayed at home to give Sue and Liz a base and some continuity and then each school holiday we'd go out to join Peter if it was suitable to do so.

I think 'busy' was an understatement of my life during those years! Selling the flat, buying a house, arranging schooling, organising all the finances, looking after ⅓ acre of garden and a general Jack of all trades!! As for Peter, his life was one of constantly moving, adapting, being on his own, missing his two little girls and earning the money to keep us all going. How lucky we were to be able to fly out in the school holidays to join him for at least a short stay. When we weren't overseas we were doing 'normal' things at home with the occasional day out.

A day out at Stonehenge 1964 in the days before it was cordoned off

Christmas and New Year (62/63) the girls and I spent at the flat. It was the winter of the 'Big Freeze'. Snow drifts were over six foot high and getting around for many weeks was very difficult. Power cuts were frequent and keeping warm meant sitting in front of an open oven door with the gas on!

We put the flat on the market and whilst Peter was away I sold it and on one of his trips home we found a house in Hartley Wintney. I must admit to being a little naughty when selling the flat. A prospective buyer came to view and really liked it but was hesitant in committing. So I mentioned that someone else was coming to look at it. This focused his mind as he didn't want to lose it and he made an offer. What I omitted to mention was that the other person coming to view was in fact another estate agent!

Romney Cottage

We then had to organise transferring the mortgage to 'Romney Cottage' – our find in Hartley Wintney, and Peter was only home for a few days. In those days the process was slightly more complicated and required more personal data. We had to arrange to meet the Sun Life rep in the car park at the local pub on a Sunday for Peter to have a 'medical'. This consisted of him being weighed on a portable weighing machine and his height measured against the outside wall of the pub! The documents were signed and all was arranged; we had bought Romney Cottage for £5,700 (in 1963)!! It was one of three 1930's houses, beyond the common planted with oak trees and at the beginning of a bridle track. The walk into the village was past the oak trees, which had been planted by Lady Milmay around 1821 when William Cobbett rode by on his travels. On the left was a wooden village hall which was used for local meetings and jumble sales. I still have a large turkey dish I bought there for 3 old pence! Nearby was the village pond and The Cricketers pub. The A30 ran through the shopping area with most of these shops having been taken over by the antique trade over the years. On our side of the main road was a prep school, the Grey House, which both girls attended.

Liz at the Grey House school aged 5

During our first year there Peter went on temporary postings to Tokyo (during build up to the 1964 Olympics) and Johannesburg. Then in December he was sent to Rio de Janeiro and here we joined him for the Christmas holidays. He was staying at an hotel – The Trocadero – overlooking the Copacabana beach. It was a very pleasant hotel, although it did have a bit of a reputation, as it was the hotel where Ronald Biggs, the train robber had stayed. The beach is very impressive; a deep expanse of sand edged with the very distinctive black and white 'harlequin' tiled pavements. The beach was always busy with people sunbathing, surfing, kite-flying and playing beach volley ball. Sue and Liz were very excited about staying in a 'posh' hotel and having their own room with en-suite facilities! On arrival they rushed around playing with every gadget in the room and turned on every tap in the bathroom. There was a water cut at the time so no water appeared, and as we were unable to have a shower to freshen up we went out for a meal. On returning to the hotel there was much commotion in the corridor outside our rooms. It would appear that soon after we had left the hotel the water supply had been reconnected and as the girls had left all the taps 'on' including the spray setting on the bidet, their bathroom was awash! One helpful chambermaid, many towels and an hour later all was resolved.

Apart from playing on the beach while Peter was at work, on one of his days off we took the funicular railway up to see the Corcovado; a huge and very impressive statue of Christ with outstretched arms in the form of a cross. We also went to the Sugar Loaf Mountain, the other iconic landmark in Rio. However our short holiday went by quickly with only one other memorable event! One evening during our stay Liz suddenly came out in a most alarming rash which apparently irritated immensely. There was nothing for it but to ask the hotel to call for a doctor. He duly arrived, quite late in the evening, and diagnosed an allergic rash and gave us a prescription. Peter then had to get a taxi to try and find the 'duty' chemist that was open at midnight with his few words of Portugese and a taxi driver who spoke no English! He succeeded while the girls and I stayed at the hotel playing 'Donkey' trying to distract Liz from scratching her spots! Donkey must have been the current favourite game to have been included in our luggage! The next day Liz was still not feeling very bright and not feeling at all like eating but Peter sat Liz on his shoulders and carried her through the streets to our favourite restaurant, a Rodizio. This was a typical Brazilian restaurant, specialising in meat often served on skewers which were cooked on an open fire. While we ordered our lunch all Liz wanted was a Coca Cola. Then I suddenly remembered. When we were living in Bahrain some friends of ours had had a very young baby about 5/6 weeks old who became very sick and could not keep anything down at all not even water and so was quickly becoming dehydrated, a very serious situation in such a hot climate. Their normal doctor was away so they saw the locum who was a local Arab doctor who had recently returned from his training in the States. His recommendation to these desperate parents was to give the baby Coca Cola! They did and the baby kept it down and soon recovered! So Liz had her glass of Coke and in no time at all she'd shaken off her lethargy and was running around bright as ever! Coca Cola has been a family 'cure' ever since although I think the recipe has changed since those days!!

Peter's posting to Rio was originally only meant to be for 3 weeks but was eventually extended, week by week, month by month until in the end his stay lasted 11 months. During the months that followed our Christmas visit the political scenario became tense with a general strike and the threat of civil war. Peter wrote:

"All the banks are closed until next Monday at the earliest. No buses or trams and I believe that the railways are on strike. According to the papers the coal for the gas supplies will only last another day..... There was panic buying at the food shops this morning, and long queues at all food shops selling tinned goods. Nobody knows what is going to happen, and all the radios are out, except the national radio, and nobody believes what they are saying. It's all one big mess. Our aircraft which usually comes north this afternoon has been held in Montevideo and may operate via Lima. I am in the town office taking care of communications here. Everybody else has gone home. Everything is quiet though......."

Peter didn't get any further with his writing for at that moment he heard a row outside the office and he opened the door. He continued:-

"The shutters were down thank goodness, and there was a fellow with a revolver in his hand, not pointing it at me, but then an ugly mob started hurling stones at this fellow. You see the Military Club is just next door, and they were aiming at that, not BOAC, but we caught the rocks against our shutters. Then the shooting started and someone was hit just outside our door. More rocks pelted our shutters and firing. In the beginning there were no police around at all, but then some came with fixed bayonets. The situation was rather ugly for an hour or so and then I went upstairs into the Military Club and got out later on. ....

Everything is back to normal now......it could have been very nasty, but all is well now. The Presidente has gone to Montevideo and his family to Madrid and they have a new one now. Pro right wing. It has been a hard blow to the communists."

Chapter 12

Venezuela, Ceylon, Switzerland and Nigeria (1965)

Peter continued on his string of temporary postings during 1965 but my only opportunity to join him was during October when he was on a two month posting to Caracas, Venezuela. We arranged for the girls to board at their prep school while I had a two week holiday with Peter.

Caracas – Venezuela – oil – modern city – the Orinoco River – a Caribbean coastline and that's about all I knew about the place! A hurried search in our local library – and not a single book could be found to help. Plenty of literature on Brazil and a few on other South American countries but nobody seemed to have written volumes on Venezuela!

Ten days after the initial arrangements I was sitting on a balcony overlooking the Caribbean with the Andes rising steeply behind the hotel (now I didn't know that the Andes came this far north!)

Caracas Sheraton taken from the hotel brochure

Between the hotel buildings and the beach were two swimming pools. Gardens surrounded the pool areas with their gaily coloured sunloungers. The first morning, tired after the journey and a clock adjustment of 5 hours (with the subsequent upset of meal times) I leisurely passed the day and watched the equally leisurely cleaning of the pool below me. One man walked the circumference of the pool with a fishing net extracting floating leaves, then the floor of the pool was gradually 'swept' by means of ever-lengthening handles and then he dived into the pool complete with mask and the job was finished off by sweeping all towards a central drain. One man, two hours. While in the background, pelicans skimmed the water on the sea beyond finally resting on a little jetty.

The journey out had been uneventful, on a new Boeing 707 jet seating over 120 passengers. It took 7 hours and two meals to get to Bermuda, an irregular shaped island with blue sea, plenty of greenery and white houses with their white ridged roofs forming water catchment areas on this river-less island. Then more island hopping via Barbados and Trinidad before arriving at Maiquetia the coastal airport for Caracas.

The hotel, The Macuto Sheraton, was reputed to be one of the best hotels in South America. It was government subsidised and lavishly equipped. But tourism didn't seem to be encouraged at the time. As the world's largest exporter of oil and with large deposits of iron, gold and diamonds they didn't seem to need the extra income that might be generated by tourism.

I had been looking forward to my first visit to Caracas city which was 10 miles inland, the hotel and airport both being on the coast. There was a new dual carriageway which linked the airport with the capital which was a wonderful piece of engineering climbing 3,000 feet in 10 miles. Part of the road tunnels right through a small mountain and out of the other side! Caracas turned out to be a real mixture of a city with some low Spanish houses with curved tiled roofs and uneven pavements while new buildings including the impressive twin towers dominating the skyline. During our visit we discovered that Caracas was a city considerably lacking in public loos, or at least any identifiable ones, and finding that our few words of Spanish were inadequate Peter was driven to stopping someone and having to demonstrate his need! Luckily there were some nearby.

Christmas 1965 and we were out in Ceylon again, for a six week visit. The accommodation varied by posting and this time we were living in a very nice bungalow, in the suburbs of Colombo, which was the home of the airport manager (and his family) for whom Peter was covering. The family had left a lot of their personal possessions for us including linen, books, oh! – and a pet rabbit and two tortoises! As it was so close to Christmas they had also put up Christmas decorations for us, which was a very kind touch. We also 'adopted' their staff for the duration of our stay. They were Mary, the nanny, a cook called Muttiah and Manuel the house-boy. Luckily Liz took to Mary and loved the rabbit! Unfortunately during our stay however the rabbit became ill and despite a trip to the vets died just before we left. Liz was distraught.

Having been in Ceylon in the mid 50's it was interesting to see how it had changed. Sadly it seemed to have deteriorated and tourists were not encouraged; they were merely tolerated. The infrastructure was poor with the roads being particularly treacherous and not helped by the awful driving. Driving at night along the road between Colombo and the airport which was at Negombo near a small fishing village north of Colombo was a hazardous undertaking as elephants, which were still widely used as working animals and were walked on the main roads, did not have headlights or rear brake lights!

Elephants being washed at the coast with Liz [with a sunhat] and a friend

While Peter was at work the girls and I would spend time at the swimming club where Liz started her first strokes or at home, with occasional trips into Colombo itself. There was also a beach nearby belonging to the Mount Lavinia Hotel which was a popular spot. We would sometimes have a curry lunch there, and they were particularly famous for their hot fish curries which were helped a little by the addition of a sliced banana!

Although it was very hot and sticky with a large number of storms and heavy rain and despite Peter's long hours at work we did manage a few trips around the island. We went to Hikkaduwa to the south of the island travelling through the tall coconut plantations before arriving at the beach and small fishing village. We revisited Kandy in the centre of the island and again went to the 'The Temple of the Tooth'.

The lake at Kandy

Peter, Sue and Liz by Kandy Lake

This time we also went to the Botanical Gardens which were filled with an abundance of tropical fruits and spices including, cinnamon, allspice, nutmeg and sandalwood: the air was full of their scent. There were also a large number of varieties of palm trees displayed there including the Talipot Palm, one of the largest fan palms in the world. This palm only flowers once in its life generally between the ages of 30-80 and then it dies. Incredibly the Talipot palm in the gardens was in bloom! It had amazing 30ft spikes with a myriad of small yellow flowers.

We also managed to arrange a visit with another family up into the central uplands into the tea plantations. It was a five hour journey from Colombo via a short stop at Ratnapura for a picnic breakfast and then climbing on up to Haputale on narrow twisting roads. We stayed at the Monamaya guest house which was a simple, but very colonial affair, originally having been a tea planter's house.

Monamaya Rest House 1965

Although the guest house was comfortable I do remember having a very disturbed sleep as the rather large clock in the hallway chimed every hour day and night! Haputale is over four and a half thousand feet above sea level and some of the views were spectacular. The guest house was surrounded by tea plantations and the children went off exploring while the local women picked the bud and the two young leaves throwing them into the big carrier strapped to their backs.

Peter at the Tea Plantation

The children playing at the Tea Plantation

The children playing at the Tea Plantation

Sue managed to get lost on the steep hillside paths but was found before dark! The following day we clambered over the rocks by the Diyaluma Falls and went to the nearby town of Bandarawela where there was a huge mango tree in the grounds of one of the hotels. All the vegetation was very lush and tropical helped by the frequent rain and low misty clouds that would drape over these high peaks.

Returning to Colombo it was back to our day to day activities, Peter working most afternoons and evenings and the girls and I filling our days; including visits to the dentist for Sue where she had to have a broken tooth removed, visits to the vet to try and sort out the rabbit (to no avail) and friends to tea etc. etc.

Before we returned to the UK we also had a day at Ratnapura visiting the rubber plantation and factory. It was a very rudimentary process and highly labour intensive with each worker tapping 250 trees on alternate days. However the process was also heavily reliant on elephants which were trained to pull the old trees out and to do any other heavy work.

Elephants working

After a busy 6 weeks we returned to England.

At the beginning of 1966 Peter went to Zurich for two months and I was able to join him for a couple of days. We went to Davos and travelled on the train to the summit and had lunch amongst the skiers. How unusual for us to be somewhere cold. I can remember having a very tasty cheese fondue while we were there!

In the snow at Davos

By March and after a spot of leave, Peter was off to Kano, Nigeria for his next posting, where he stayed until the October. So we joined him for some time during the girls' summer holidays. We stayed in a company house and were provided with staff, as was normal, including a very fierce looking night watchman. He was a Taureg from the Sahara and was supplied, terrifyingly, with a rifle! He lived on our verandah and possessed a bicycle and a bundle of clothes.

We were there during the time of the 'Ground Nut Scheme', when the Colonial office encouraged the Nigerians to grow peanuts for the oil, which was then exported. Prior to the oil extraction the farmers piled the sacks of peanuts into huge pyramids in the fields. We did a bit of exploring around Kano including a day trip up to Kaduna.

A local bus

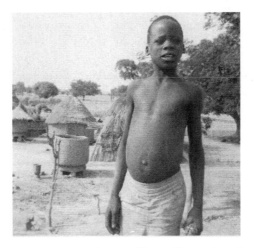

Nigerian boy standing in front of his village, Northern Nigeria

A corral of local huts, Northern Nigeria

There was a lot of civil unrest in Nigeria in the 60's. In January 1966 the military had attempted a coup d'état. Although it failed the unrest continued and in the summer of 66, after the girls and I had left, a counter coup was undertaken by the largely Christian minority Ibo tribe. The Ibo's set fire to the boundaries enclosing an Arab settlement in Kano, allowing no escape. At the airport they attacked the local staff and one of Peter's staff was shot in front of him. Others escaped through windows and stowed away onboard the aircraft. They also rounded up the passengers at gunpoint, but somehow the aircraft eventually took off with the passengers plus plenty of stowaways! Peter was commended on his handling of what had been a very difficult situation.

Chapter 13

Antigua, Aden and Barbados (1966 – 1967)

After Peter's leave in the November, which was spent enjoying Romney Cottage and living a 'normal' life he was posted to Antigua – what a pleasant change! So after a very busy time during December – visiting, entertaining, gardening and shopping – I gathered the girls together and we flew out to Antigua on December 28th. The company house where we stayed was a bungalow on the rocks on the north coast with our own tiny beach. The night we arrived the wind howled and the rain fell from the sky and the rats played 'football' on the tin roof above our heads! Thankfully the weather improved the next day and the rain water had helped to fill our water tank which we used for drinking during the long and frequent water cuts. There is no natural water on the island and the water in the taps was salt water, so the rainwater was especially valuable. Apart from the rats in the roof (which we did get the pest control folk to see to) we didn't get troubled by other insects in the house, it was just the sand flies on the beach that gave a very nasty bite of which we had to be aware. So visits to the beach to collect shells were brief and we were well covered!

In between Peter's duties at the airport we went on trips round the island – to St Johns the capital one day, which was more like a small village, and then down to the south of the island to Nelson's Dockyard at English Harbour on another. The dockyard is full of memorabilia from the days when Nelson brought his fleet into the well protected bay. Some of the stone pillars had been built with stones brought from England as ballast in the old oak sailing ships. We were talking to the harbour master when stooping to peer down a crab hole, my sunglasses slipped off my head and disappeared down the hole, way out of sight. The harbour master assured me that if I returned the next morning he would have the glasses for me, for the crabs would bring to the surface items that fell into their hole! Unfortunately we were staying the other side of the island and were unable to return to see if this was true. After having the house pointed out where

107

Princess Margaret spent her honeymoon, we drove up to Shirley Heights which has a wonderful view of the dockyard and surrounding area. Various coachloads of tourists were also enjoying the views, except one crowded with Americans. As they got off their coach they were surrounded by locals selling necklaces of local shells and beads. They spent about 10 minutes haggling and making their purchases and then reboarded their coach without a glance at the stunning surroundings! Two weeks later we flew back to wintry England, via Bermuda. Four days later the girls were back to school and we were back to 'routine'; whatever that was!

Peter came home for a week in February and then was off to Aden. While he was away, my life carried on back in the UK. Amongst my other 'occupations' when at home, I delivered 'meals on wheels' with a friend. In those days the meals were stacked in containers with a naked flame – a candle warmer to keep the meals reasonably hot and these we put in the boot of the car. On one particular day we realised that there was smoke emerging from the boot – we had nearly set the car on fire! There were some isolated old cottages in the area and the occupants were always so pleased to see us. I painted and decorated, made curtains and gardened and on Feb 25th planted broad beans!

There was another event at that time. Liz had a friend nearby called Jackie, whose family dog had just had a litter of pups. We volunteered to visit and feed the mum and her pups whilst they were away for a few days. So off we went and I opened the door and put the key on the hall table – amongst the excitement somehow or other we were all outside and the front door banged shut! So keys, hungry mother dog and puppies were locked inside! We returned home and failing to think of any way we could get in I phoned the police station and explained the situation! They said that they were unable to 'break in' to the house, but could unofficially tell me how some burglars did!! – Spread some golden syrup on a piece of brown paper and attach to the window. Then break the glass and all the shattered glass would stick to the treacly paper – not ideal but wouldn't leave too much mess! I am serious! So armed with a step stool to reach the lowest window, a roll of brown paper, a tin of Lyles Golden Syrup and a hammer the three of us walked down the road and proceeded to follow instructions. The result was a very sticky mess of shattered glass all over the net curtain and the surrounding carpet – and a not very happy family on their return! But we were able to feed the dog and puppies.

Peter's time in Aden was difficult. It was not a safe or happy place at this time. There were road blocks, armed soldiers, strikes and power cuts. Hand grenades were being thrown indiscriminately, so Peter's hotel room became his office, he being the only British BOAC staff member there at the time. Part of his job was to inspect the home-bound coffins to ensure there were no explosives hidden by terrorists to blow up the plane. I was very pleased to be at the airport to meet him on his return after 6 weeks – on my birthday!

After three weeks leave, which we spent mostly decorating, Peter was off again, this time to Calcutta, another unpleasant posting. But on this posting he had a hundred staff and was kept very busy in a hot, humid overcrowded town office as well as overseeing the arrivals and departures at Dum Dum airport. It was three months before he was home again and this time just for a week before he was off again. But to a much nicer place, Barbados, where we were able to join him for 2 weeks during the summer holidays. It was such a privilege to be able to join Peter on these occasions, conditions and school holidays permitting. We visited not as tourists but as visitors – a big difference. We usually stayed in local accommodation and had the facility of a car. We 'did' touristy things but in our own time, and we met local people often through Peter's work. When we went out to Barbados we stayed for a few days in a hotel and then we moved to an isolated bungalow at the southernmost tip of the island.

The property was rented by BOAC and owned by a local lady, whose daughter was a student in London studying ballet. Whilst talking to the owner one day we discovered that her daughter was living in a rented bed-sit, which, on further questioning, turned out to have been Peter's bedroom when he was a young boy!! His grandfather had owned three adjacent three storey houses in Willesden, the family lived in the central one and those on either side were rented out. After the houses were eventually sold they were turned into bedsits as were many of the larger houses in London. What an amazing coincidence linking Peter's childhood days to this property thousands of miles away.

The bungalow was accessed through fields of sugar cane and situated by a long isolated beach. There was also a marshy area which attracted wild fowl, but unfortunately wild fowl hunters as well! Whilst Peter was on duty we swam and collected shells, read and played games. In the evening we would lie on our backs on the patio star gazing at a clear sky in complete isolation with little, if any, artificial light to contaminate the view! The Milky Way was so clear you felt that you could reach out your hand and touch it. But not all was idyllic, when it rained (which it often did) it noisily bounced off the tin roof, the rain brought out the mosquitoes and at about 5am we would wake to the sound of the wild fowl hunters starting to shoot!! On Peter's days off we went into Bridgetown and had flying fish for lunch and visited Pelican Village, a tourist set up of shops and cafes. We went to Sam Lords Castle which was an imposing house on the southern coast full of antiques and being run as an upmarket hotel. (Sadly this beautiful building was destroyed by fire in 2010.) We also drove up to the North Shore Surf Club and returned via Bathsheba, a small town perched on the east coast and approached by a perilously steep downhill road. The North and East coasts bore the full brunt of the Atlantic winds and seas and the coastline was rocky and the rolling surf attracted surfers. The calm sandy beaches of the West and Southern shores however, provided a mecca for the majority of the tourists seeking luxury hotels and a quiet spot in which to sun bathe. After two weeks we returned as the school holidays were coming to an end.

After a wonderful holiday we were reminded on the return journey that staff travel has its disadvantages. We were offloaded in the middle of the night as the plane transited in Bermuda. With two young children, this is no fun! We eventually returned to the UK after 24 hours in Bermuda, to an overgrown garden and preparations for a new term at school. Autumn passed by with minor ups and downs and general business – household chores, gardening, homework, school activities and chutney making! After coming home for a spell of leave Peter was off again back to Ceylon – for the third time! He left just before the end of the year (1967) missing the snow at home and also Sue's 13th birthday in early January.

Chapter 14

Ceylon and N. Ireland (1968)

We went up to London for Sue's birthday – some shopping, a Chinese lunch and then saw Tommy Steele in 'Half a Sixpence' before returning back home to Hartley Wintney. I tried to take Sue and Liz up to London for outings during the holidays. One time we went to 'do' Carnaby Street and on another we went to one of Robert Meyer's classical concerts for children at the Albert Hall. We would often end up in the Pathe News cinema on Waterloo station just to fill in the odd half an hour. Later in January we had more snow and I slithered around delivering meals on wheels. I seem to have done a lot of knitting, tapestry and sewing that winter. I made most of the girls' clothes and some of mine, as was quite normal. They always had pants matching their dresses!! I was also doing a course in English Literature!

We went to Ceylon, for the third time, during the Easter holidays in April for two weeks and joined Peter in the company house in the suburbs of the capital Colombo. It was very hot but we were able to go swimming most days. We also took Sue to her first 'night-club'! We went for dinner at The Mount Lavinia Hotel with some of Peter's colleagues. Sue had had a dress made for her from a blue, floral silk fabric and she felt very grown up and glamorous! The DJ in the night club played a few records while they were setting up so that she and her friend Stephen could have a dance! However we were soon back to normality! We travelled home via Karachi and Rome and were met by family at the airport and driven home to Hampshire – what a quick change in climate and environment! After a few days of re-adjusting, the girls were back at school and I was back to Heathrow to pick up Peter on his return!

Then what a contrast: Peter's next posting was Belfast! Here the accommodation provided was a caravan in the middle of a field sharing it with a herd of cows! His departure from the UK was delayed as his luggage was stolen from our roof rack when we stopped for lunch en route to the airport. We returned to the multi-storey car park to find the luggage gone. So after filing insurance claims and sourcing a new uniform he was on his way. I managed a few days there, not the most palatial of living conditions, sleeping in sleeping bags, but it did enable us to visit the Giants Causeway. Most of the time that Peter was in Belfast (nearly 3 months) he came home for the weekends, so I became even more familiar with the A30, doing the round trip from Hartley Wintney to the airport in about 3hrs, twice a week! In the meantime Sue had passed her 11 plus and had moved on from the prep school in the village, the Grey House, to the girls' grammar school in Basingstoke.

I had a worrying time one evening. Sue was on a float in the Basingstoke Carnival. They had all dressed up as football supporters and were using a neighbour's milk lorry as the float vehicle. When she hadn't arrived home at the expected hour, I got very worried and phoned the police. It turned out that while the lorry had been going round a roundabout on the A30, just heading into Basingstoke, the strut that Sue was leaning on had given way and she had done a backward somersault onto the main road. As she didn't appear to be hurt, apart from grazing her nose, the driver put her into the passenger seat in the cab and continued to take part in the procession! Luckily after a few days rest with some delayed shock and a visit to the doctors, who diagnosed strained neck muscles, she recovered and was soon back to normal!

Chapter 15

India (1968)

After visits to the Caribbean and to Northern Ireland the next excitement was two visits to a very contrasting part of the world – Delhi, India. I went by myself for two weeks in October and then all three of us went over the Christmas holidays. From plum picking, jam and chutney making and blackberrying in the country lanes, I arrived in Delhi early October to join Peter in the company flat. It was spacious, occupying two floors with a verandah overlooking a very busy main road next door to the zoo! There were several British staff and I was immediately absorbed into the 'overseas life' of coffees, lunches and cocktail parties! As for the latter, notes made at the time after an Air France cocktail party read:-   " Pleasant temperature – carpets laid on the lawn – trays of drinks – very interesting food and met the Pan Am manager with broken collar bone!"

We had lunches at the Oberoi Hotel, visited the zoo and one evening went to the Red Fort for a 'Son et Lumiere'. The Red Fort, in old Delhi, is built of red sandstone, a massive and very impressive structure built by Shah Jehan which took nine years to build in the 17th century. Shah Jehan is better known for building the Taj Mahal in Agra in loving memory of his beloved wife, Mumtaz. In 1638 he moved the capital of India from Agra to Delhi. One day during our stay a driver picked us up and we went to Agra to see the Taj Mahal. The journey was interesting; through local villages but the sight of the Taj itself is most impressive. We walked through the main gate and past the seat (since made famous by Princess Diana) along the garden by the water features. Entering the massive building with its intricately inset coloured stones and gems and incredible workmanship was indeed to visit one of the world's most amazing buildings.

The following day was the Festival of Diwali which was celebrated with colourful fireworks and lighted candles. But during the day we went to the see the Qutub Minar.

This is a 236ft tower with projecting balconies over 800 years old. It is in Delhi and is the tallest monument in India built as a victory tower by the Moghuls. Internally there are 378 steps with access to the balconies. At the time of our visit the climb to the top was restricted as there had recently been too many suicides from the balconies. Nearby is the Iron Pillar. This again is a very impressive structure of great interest to geologists, archeologists and corrosion technologists as it has stood around 1800 years and shows no signs of corrosion or rust!

(As you may have gathered by now, we were always keen to visit any places of interest whilst on our travels, unlike some people we knew who spent 6 months in Cairo and never bothered to visit the Pyramids!)

Old Delhi consists of narrow streets and was noisy, smelly and overpopulated. Many craftsmen lived and worked in tiny open workshops while rattling old motor vehicles, donkey drawn carts and rickshaws with motor cycle engines competed with the throngs of people for space on the dusty roads.

In market areas like this in Eastern countries there was a distinctive shaped brass coffee pot with a large spout. However in the markets in Delhi, Tibetan coffee pots were available which were larger and more ornate. During Peter's stay there he purchased several and we soon discovered that by putting one in our local auction room at home (Fleet) we were able to make enough profit to pay for a term's school fees!

After two weeks of the house boy bringing in a tray of 'bed-tea' for Sahib and Memsahib and pulling back the curtains, I was up early and off to the airport. After a long flight home via Bahrain and Kuwait (which was delayed en route consequently 9hrs between breakfast and lunch!) I arrived home hungry and tired and back to my 'other world' of shopping, cleaning, cooking, catching up with friends and family until the next time. On Guy Fawkes Night we went to a firework party at a friend's house and there was a bonfire on the common.

By the middle of December all three of us were on a flight to Delhi for Christmas – staying in the flat which was all new to Sue and Liz. Again many busy days, visits to the zoo, entertaining and being entertained, shopping and parties.

One day there was great activity on a piece of land adjacent to our flat. A team of people spent a continuous 24hrs making an archway of garlands of marigolds. It soon became apparent that this was for a wedding celebration. A marquee was erected and the groom arrived on his white stallion, staying for about 10 minutes before proceeding to the main ceremony.

Donald Milner, the long term BBC correspondent for Delhi, lived nearby and the girls were invited to their children's Christmas party. One day we went by car with another family for a day's drive down to Agra. Peter was working this time, but we took a picnic which we ate in the gardens of the Taj Mahal. We visited the Qutub Minar again and explored some more of Delhi. We saw in the New Year (1969) quietly with champagne on the verandah, then on 3 January, the day before Sue's birthday a group of us had dinner at the Oberoi restaurant and the orchestra played 'Happy Birthday' much to Sue's delight! (Sue was 14 and Liz nearly 10) The following day was the Junior Jet Club party. The Jet Club was for school children who regularly commuted from boarding schools to their parents overseas for the school holidays. I remember I had to give out prizes – but I'm not sure what for! The following day we all left for home. Again the aircraft was delayed for 5 hours in Teheran and when we eventually arrived in London we had to wait 2 hours for our luggage (some things never change!).

Chapter 16

Jamaica (1969)

Spring 1969: another big change in lifestyle with lots of arrangements to be made. Elizabeth was now 10 and so both girls were old enough to go to boarding school. There were about 6 schools on our list that were known to take daughters of families whose parents worked overseas. We eliminated some, and then one of the remaining possibilities hit the headlines with a story of 'Headmaster's affair with 6th form girl'! Somehow we didn't think that was such a good idea so we chose one in Hindhead, Surrey, where they started at the beginning of April.

So having sorted that, I was free to join Peter who had left for Montego Bay earlier that month on a more 'permanent' posting and I became a full-time ex-pat's wife again. Full time if one allows for returns home for half-terms and then home again for annual leaves! After Peter left I had to get the house cleared and cleaned and ready for letting and all that that entailed. During this time we had a violent thunderstorm and the house was struck by lightning. I was in the kitchen at the time and felt the 'strike' going around and 'hitting' the hot water pipe behind the boiler, which then spouted out boiling water. Luckily I had a helpful dentist (his profession however being quite irrelevant to this incident!!) neighbour who came around and turned off the water supply. I felt shaken for several days and had no water, no gas and no telephone! Somehow one sort of copes on these occasions. Before I left there was a Parents Day and half term at the school. The girls came home for the half term break and then three days later I was on the aircraft bound for Montego Bay (or Mo Bay as it was affectionately known) with 91 kgs of luggage!!

It was the rainy season in Jamaica when I arrived. Hot and sticky and loads of mosquitoes. Peter was covering the operation at Kingston as well, so constantly commuting by air. This meant he was able to leave me the car which however kept breaking down; back to overseas life!

The rain kept coming and a tap kept leaking. Eventually after 3 weeks a plumber arrived with a book entitled 'How to Plumb' in his hand saying "only take 15 minutes"! Three hours later he left saying "will come back" and left us with no water at all!

One of our tea chests must have been dropped on the way there as all our china was broken (for the second time); so then began the insurance claims. Eventually the rains eased off and the girls arrived for their summer holidays. We explored the south and east coasts nearest to Mo Bay. Negril on the west coast was the most beautiful and deserted stretch of beach about 1½ hours' drive away. Now it is full of hotels and hippies! Another enjoyable outing along the coast eastwards was Dunns River Falls at Ocho Rios where Sue and Liz climbed up the 630ft of the falls with a guide.

Mo Bay was a very social spot and with numerous airline and hotel managers we entertained at our homes and met up for drinks at Doctors Cave, the local beach club. The sea was clear and deep and there were two diving platforms anchored a little way off the shoreline with a bar conveniently on the beach. So still and clear was the water in the calm season that a friend who lost a ring whilst out on one of the platforms found it the following day, 6ft down lying on top of the sand! Once a month on a Sunday a steel band played which was always a popular event.

Letters and notes from Mo Bay that summer seem to emphasize the lack of water, a very unreliable car, lots of heavy rain, a near miss by a hurricane, Peter commuting between the two island's airports and lots of letter writing (72 at one count!). On the day that Neil Armstrong landed on the moon (July 20th), we explored the caves at Runaway Bay a drive of about 40 miles along the coast. It was so called after the slaves working on the neighbouring sugar plantations escaped and hid there. While there we went around an underground lake on a small boat. That same evening we went to a friend's house for an Italian meal – never a dull moment!

One of the couples we met was the local Methodist minister and his wife. His 'patch' was a very large one and on one of his trips inland to see his parishioners he invited the girls and me to accompany him. This involved quite a long drive to the central part of the island known as the Cockpit country which had provided a refuge for the Maroons; 'cimarrones' was the Spanish for runaway slaves. This was a very hilly area to where many slaves made their way after escaping from the sugar estates. It was rugged country with many caves and was easily defended. It seems strange these days to be talking of 'slaves' but in fairly recent history most of the workers on the large sugar estates were men and women 'imported' from Africa. The land owners were mostly British and lived in the Great Houses; the remnants of which are scattered over the island. Maroon Town, the regional centre, is about ¾hr from Mo Bay and it was a fascinating ride. Just as we left Mo Bay the road turned inland and standing on a hill in a very commanding position was the house which used to belong to Lord Beaverbrook and just around the bend in the road is Parson's Bridge, named after the fact that a parson crashed into it! Then we soon passed the entrance to The Salvation Army School for the Blind, the only school for the blind on the island. They looked after hundreds of blind boys who ran a poultry farm on their own along with other mentally and physically handicapped boys. The general facilities available for the care of handicapped people in Jamaica were very limited and so this was a rare example where the boys were well cared for and where they could make a useful contribution to society and be independent.

The road climbed higher into the hilly districts and it was here that the bananas flourished. At several points along the road there were 'boxing' stations. These open sided sheds were collecting points for the bunches of bananas which arrived very green and were stacked amongst dried leaves until they were cut into 'hands', washed, dried and packed in cardboard containers, which were being stapled together on the spot. Those containers when fully packed held about 30lbs of bananas. These were then loaded on to lorries and then onto banana boats, mainly Fyffes in those days, to England.

When we reached the outskirts of Maroon Town there were many cars and plenty of people gathered outside the doctor's surgery. He was apparently very well-known and people came from many neighbouring villages to see him. Meanwhile the minister introduced us to a Mr Tapper and his wife and we stayed in their house whilst he made some calls. Mr Tapper was a great talker. He was 84 and recalled his childhood clearly. He came to live in his present house when he was 6 and his father was a farmer. He showed us coffee and cocoa growing in his garden. He cut us some lovely pineapples and hands of bananas to take home with us and included a pack of the solid cocoa which you grate to use. He and his wife recalled the early days of the century when roads were mere tracks, when there were just a few horse and buggies and no other transport. It was not until 1930 that any roads were

*A PanAm plane
flying across
Doctors Cave
Beach,
Montego Bay*

*At Doctors Cave Beach,
Montego Bay*

*Peter and Francis (Peter's
cousin) on Doctors Cave
beach drinking
the local Red Stripe beer)*

My class,
Montego Bay

Rose hall,
Jamaica

The view from Rose hall
looking over the sea.

With the girls about to fly to Kingston, Jamaica

Gladstone cutting down coconuts with Muriel, in our garden in Montego Bay

Peter and the girls and Yvonne and John (Peter's sister and nephew) enjoying drinking the coconut water.

Our house in Muthaiga, Nairobi

The New Stanley Hotel with the acacia tree growing out of The Thorn Tree Café, Nairobi

Artistic impression of the Norfolk Hotel, Nairobi

made up. In 1912 a building committee, including Mr Tapper and his father, was formed to collect money to build the new Methodist Church. They hoped for contributions from a rich resident in Falmouth, but he said he would only help them if they helped themselves so they collected £50 in six months which he matched giving them £100 in total. They then collected another £50 during the following six months which he again matched, so they managed to collect £200 in a year.

Mr and Mrs Tapper were both pale skinned and fair haired like many of the inhabitants of Maroon Town. This was due to the 'extra- curricular activities' of the British soldiers explained the Minister! British troops were stationed up there during the time of the rebellion following the emancipation of the slaves. The agreement was that the slaves, after being freed, would continue to spend two years working for their former owners before moving on. This was a not a quick enough 'release' for many of them and they fled to the Cockpit Country. Troops were sent to bring them back, but as they were unable to do so their freedom was eventually recognised and they were allowed to stay in their own territory. Today their descendants continue to inhabit this jealously guarded unofficial state. They pay no taxes, conduct their own judicial system and permission must be obtained to enter their country. In return they agree to fight on behalf of Jamaica should the need arise! Near to Maroon Town, is the settlement of Flagstaff, named after the flagpole of the troops stationed there and there is a graveyard of British soldiers by the side of the road. Unevenly placed on a green hillock are 26 tombstones all identical, only two with any inscription; one a soldier who died in 1840, the other a wife of a soldier, Hilary, who died in 1846. The road finished in this tiny village of one shop.

Much of my time was taken up with finding more shells for my collection. Unfortunately I don't have much left of my large collection – having shipped it around the world in packing cases for several years. I also seem to have spent a lot of time dressmaking for myself and the girls.

At the end of August we returned from an afternoon on the beach, which had been hot and sunny, the best for a while, and a drive back home at sunset. When Peter got home he received a phone call from the Station Engineer who said that he'd been watching TV and seen a report of a tropical storm approaching Kingston from the S. East. Peter immediately checked with the met office in Kingston who confirmed that Tropical Storm Francelia was expected to hit the island. So we hurriedly had supper, cleared the surfaces of ornaments that might become missiles in a high wind, opened up the louvred windows to allow any wind to go through the house and clutching supplies of candles and matches headed off to the airport as Peter had to deal with an incoming flight. Although we got the backlash, the actual storm veered away from the island at the last minute. The flights however were disrupted and left a backlog of passengers at Montego Bay trying to get off the island. Because of this, when the girls were due to go back to school a few days later, we had to send them via New York. However, contrary to the company rules for unaccompanied minors they were 'offloaded' in New York...but they seemed to survive!!

Later in the year we were home for leave in a rented flat in Shoreham. We visited Peter's aunt in Devon and his Uncle in Antwerp. (Peter had been born in Antwerp and his family tree went back to the Norman Conquest, but his family had suffered much in the two world wars.)

We were back in Jamaica for Christmas. One day we visited Lisa Salmon who encouraged humming birds into her garden way up in the hills outside Montego Bay. It was an amazing place with containers of sugar syrup to encourage her array of brightly iridescent visitors.

Chapter 17

Jamaica (1970)

The following year (1970) started with a casual conversation in a queue in the bank. I was talking to Evelyn (the Methodist Minister's wife) and discovered that her friend who was headmistress of the local prep school (officially The Preparatory School in the Diocese of Jamaica) was desperate to fill the post of a teacher for her eight and nine year olds....about 26 of them. Always ready to accept a challenge I applied for a work permit and started teaching the whole range of subjects to a variety of nationalities on their way to 11+ standards back in the UK. I wish I could remember all the countries which were represented – but I can't, but they did include English, Canadian, American, Chinese and Jamaican. I taught all day and covered everything from P.E. to R.E., maths to history and English to art. Needless to say it was hard but rewarding work although I was usually only one day ahead of the children, having mugged up the day before for the following day's lessons! They were a lovely and appreciative group and when, after a year, we left Jamaica, it was a sad day.

But of course life continued outside school and late in January the Ladies English Cricket team arrived to play some matches. Several of us ex-pats were asked to act as 'hosts' and consequently we had two of the team staying with us for a few days. We dined them and ferried them around and they consumed a lot of beer!! Their Captain was Rachael Heyhoe Flint. On leaving, all the 'hosts' were presented with a souvenir teaspoon from London!! They then had the cheek to give Peter several postcards to post home (the things we did for passengers in those days!) at the airport with the message: "Had a lovely time considering it was all free!"!!!

We had a lot of rainy and stormy weather that winter considering it was meant to be 'the Season'. Most hotels closed during the summer for Hurricane season.

Our company car must have been a very clapped out version considering the number of punctures and break downs it suffered...or maybe it was just the state of the roads!

We visited Bay Roc hotel frequently which was managed by Robin Wills, a member of the cigarette family, and met many of the guests, two of whom were Stanley Holloway and his wife. Peter would collect English newspapers left on the aircraft and keep them supplied.

During the Easter holidays we visited several places on the coast. Tryall was an adapted 'Great House' on a hill with golf course and a private beach accessed by a tunnel under the road. Rose Hall, a ruin of a sugar estate Great House and haunted by the 'White Witch' (although now a luxury hotel), was towards the east along the coast road; while Fisherman's Inn, at Falmouth, was owned by a lone English woman. Here you could get lovely lobster meals and stand on the jetty watching the sea which was illuminated by phosphorescence after dark.

We also fitted in a day trip to Kingston.

There was a lot of entertaining to fit into the evenings after school. On one occasion I prepared eats and drinks for 40 on the occasion of a visit by a 'senior' manager and his wife from London. Peter's sister, Yvonne and her husband Francis and son John also came out to stay.

It was about this time that the maid, Vicky, left to have a baby and she was replaced by another maid called Muriel. We also employed a garden boy who we 'shared' with our neighbours, a friendly couple; the husband worked for the Tourist Board and his Chinese wife called Icey. One day, out of the blue, Icey called me and asked if I had a garnet ring! Which I did, a lovely 3 stone ring which Peter had had made for me in Ceylon. She said are you sure you still have it? On checking I realised that it was missing. Icey said, "Gladstone is wearing it": Gladstone being the grand name for our shared gardener. We called the police who took him away in handcuffs and my ring as evidence. I then realised that other things had gone missing recently, money and my camera amongst them. It was a while after Muriel and Gladstone had been dismissed that I also realised that one of each implement from our canteen of stainless steel cutlery was missing. It took several months before I recovered the ring from the police. This ring was later one of the many, valuable and interesting pieces of jewellery from our world-wide travels to be stolen in a burglary after we retired in Dorset.

I left Mo Bay in August and I was back at Romney Cottage in Hartley Wintney doing all the 'UK' things, visiting and entertaining friends and relations and generally catching up. Peter's aunt Nell in Devon died and I had a few days down there. Nell had been a talented artist and submitted a work to the R.A.. Unfortunately it was not accepted. At the beginning of the war she had been teaching English in Holland and spent most of the war years in a detention camp in Holland

In the school holidays we went for country walks and blackberrying. However during that summer Sue had the opportunity to go to Tehran for a holiday. It was quite an experience for her as she went to stay with a school friend who happened to be the Shah's niece. She led a very extravagant lifestyle for a few weeks being chauffeur driven around Tehran and flying by helicopter and private jet to other parts of the country – but she soon came back down to earth on her return!

Later Peter joined me at home and when the girls were back at school we went to Copenhagen for a few days. A lovely city and although unfortunately the Tivoli Gardens were closed there was plenty left to explore. We went by hydrofoil to Malmo in Sweden for an afternoon and returned on the ferry, a lovely experience. We did a tour of the castles including Elsinor and had a smorgasbord lunch. The next day we were home again.

After returning to Montego Bay for Xmas and completing another term teaching I reluctantly gave in my notice as Peter had been posted to Nairobi, Kenya; another country to be experienced.

Before leaving we had a farewell party for over 90 and I had packed 24 tea chests!

We had some leave at home before Peter left for Nairobi in September and I followed in the November. Whilst at home, Romney Cottage was sold and we cleared our mortgage and started negotiating the purchase of a smaller 'new build' house on Shoreham Beach on the Sussex coast. It was supposed to be the up and coming place approached by a bridge from Shoreham 'proper'.

Chapter 18

Kenya (1971 – 1975)

On my arrival in Nairobi in November (1971) Peter was installed in a company house, complete with house boy and shamba (gardener), in Muthaiga a wealthy suburb where many of the Embassies and High Commissions were located. Peter was manager for BOAC at the very busy airport Embakazi and worked long hours. He bought me a little Volkswagen Beetle as a run-around. However it had seen better days and getting up a hill was always a scary time wondering if it would make it to the top. It stalled a few times on busy roads when I had no idea where I was!!

For the first few months I was leading a double life: part company wife and part overseer of the purchase of our new home in England again without the aid of computers, emails, mobile phones – but I couldn't have done it without my mother's help and a few commutes home by staff travel! Anyone would have thought that it was a mansion instead of a small beach house, by the problems that I had with the builders. I eventually moved in in the February (1972).

Peter and I both settled into our new lifestyle, although we both found the altitude of 5,500ft a little difficult to get used to at first. But we did acclimatise to this and our new environment in no time at all. Nairobi became my favourite posting although it was an exhausting one for Peter and we made several life-long friends during our time there, which ended up being less than two years.

Nairobi was very busy socially with both official and personal engagements; cocktail parties were very much in vogue! There was a large ex-pat community and also a large number of old established families who were the original 'settlers' from the UK and other parts of Europe so it was a very colonial atmosphere. Some of the socialising took place in the several sports and social clubs that were very much a part of the Nairobi scene. We had a corporate membership of the Muthaiga Club, not far from our house.

The mother of a friend of ours was a member and on meeting her and delivering a small parcel we met a few other members. The day I arrived in Nairobi Peter took me to dinner at the New Stanley Hotel in town. Later I discovered that it was renowned for its café called the Thorn Tree, popular with ex-pats and travellers alike. In the centre grew a large Acacia (which gave the Thorn Tree its name), tall and spreading wide to give some pleasant shade. The feature which made the Thorn Tree different was the notice board which surrounded the trunk of the tree. Here it was the custom to leave messages for friends, often fellow travellers, and it was commonplace to say, 'If you want to find out where I am I'll leave a message on the Thorn Tree.' My memories of that night however were of the wonderful gallery that we walked passed with a selection of paintings of elephants and old steam trains painted by the celebrated artist David Shepherd.

Another favourite haunt of the ex-pats was the Norfolk Hotel. It had been the gathering place for the old time British settlers; the planters, the engineers and the members of the government since it opened on Christmas Day 1904. The main bar inside the hotel was called the Lord Delamere after Lord Delamere of the Happy Valley set. There was also a large terrace to the front of the hotel and the tables there could have told a tale or two! Having a drink at sun-down was a very colonial thing to do.

Another novelty to us were the 'Drive-in' cinemas, where you could sit comfortably in the car under the stars watching a movie on a large outdoor screen while the sound was beamed in via a loudspeaker unit that was attached to the window. We would either take a picnic or buy fried chicken from the local stalls. Families with young children would bring their little ones already dressed in their pyjamas so that they could curl up on the back seat when it all got too much for them.

Soon after we arrived, on Dec 1st, BOAC took over the handling of its own aircraft at the airport in readiness for the arrival of the Jumbo jets (Boeing 747) which were to be the first on the African continent. There were official parties to celebrate the inauguration of the first flights which arrived on December 11th and much press coverage of the event. The arrival of the Jumbo was greeted by many local dignitaries including President Kenyatta (who had a very firm handshake according to Peter!) and many hundreds of locals who ended up on the tarmac surrounding the aircraft at one point.

The rigorous security measures of today were unheard of then and people were curious about this huge new aircraft. There were 10 scheduled flights a week (five north and five south) and each aircraft had two 1st class cabins and three 2nd class. A spiral staircase led to a 'Club in the Sky' for 1st class passengers, while the economy class seat cushion was 2" wider than any previous BOAC seat. (In case you were interested!)

Sue and Liz had arrived on the 8th Dec so helped with the Xmas preparations. We did some sightseeing and had a staff party. They came with us to a New Year's Eve party and were due to return to the UK on Jan11th – but the day before chaos started at the airport! The aircraft travelling south needed an engine change at Nairobi but unfortunately the replacement being flown from London was needed at Rome where it had stopped on the way out as one of the engines of the 'carrier' plane became unserviceable! So another flight left London; in the meantime the flight travelling north from Johannesburg also arrived! Unfortunately Embakazi airport was only built to accommodate one Jumbo at a time. As you can imagine we didn't see much of Peter at this time. He was exhausted – Nairobi had turned into a very busy airport and when he eventually left the following year he was replaced by three staff; two new posts having been created to cover the work load.

Whenever we did have spare time we would explore the country and take every opportunity to see some of the wild life. So we managed some short visits to several places during our stay. Taking the road northwest out of Nairobi you travel towards the Rift Valley and Lake Naivasha is usually the first stop.

The hotel there was an attractive old colonial style building with lawns stretching down to the lake. It had been built in the late 1930's and had been used as a 'staging post' for the passengers and crew on the Imperial Airways flying boats that would be en route between London and Durban. They always put on a good Sunday lunch buffet which we ate on the lawn in the shade of the large acacia trees. The lake itself was full of wildlife – plenty of fish and birds and you could hire a boat for fishing or just to watch the powerful fish eagles swoop from their perches amongst many other colourful birds. The lake of around 100 sq. miles is situated on the floor of the Rift Valley and is surrounded by the Aberdare Mountain range and the extinct volcano of Mount Longonot. As it is only about 50 miles from Nairobi on a tarmac road it was an easy 'outing' and we went several

The first BOAC Jumbo
to land in Africa

Peter and the girls at a
craft stall on the Rift
Valley Road, Kenya

Lake Naivasha Hotel, Kenya

The girls at the entrance to The Outspan Hotel, Kenya

On the terrace of The Outspan Hotel

Overlooking elephants at the watering-hole, Voi Safari Lodge, Kenya

Ndege House,
Karen,
Nairobi

Lions in Nairobi
Game Park

Our house in Harbour Mews,
Nassau

Peter – happy in his garden in Dorset

A family photo: Liz, me, Peter and Sue

times. On one occasion we went further north to Lake Nakuru and had a picnic by the water's edge. This was a different kind of lake, wilder, with flocks of pink flamingos thriving in the alkaline water.

We visited Thika and Chania Falls. Lying to the N.E of Nairobi Thika is the spot where Elspeth Huxley's family settled in the early days and started a coffee plantation, all beautifully described in her book The Flame Trees of Thika.

Another trip was to Nyeri the home of the famous Tree Tops Hotel with its 'base' of the Outspan Hotel. We visited The Outspan and had drinks on the terrace and a wonderful lunch, but never made it to Tree Tops. The original Outspan hotel had only four bedrooms, but by 1928 there were ten rooms with private bathrooms. The owners, the Walkers, who had the hotel built, offered a bottle of champagne to whoever could suggest the best name for the hotel. The bottle was won by a neighbour who suggested "The Outspan" based on a South African word for the place where, at the end of a long day, a traveller outspans the weary oxen and camps for the night.

Tree Tops was the idea of Walker's wife, Lady Beattie, based on memories of a childhood tree-house. Built around 1930 the first house consisted of just two rooms in a fig tree. By the time Prince Philip and Princess Elizabeth visited it had grown to 3 bedrooms, a dining room and a small room for a hunter. In 1954, soon after the royal visit the original Treetops was burnt down by the Mau-Mau, but a new larger Treetops was completed in 1957 on the opposite side of the watering hole. Since then it has been extended, enlarged and changed hands several times.

Sherbrooke Walker, the original owner, had been Lord Baden-Powell's first scout commissioner and private secretary during the S. African wars. Later in the Second World War he joined the RAF and was an intelligence officer on the Northern Frontier of Kenya. His friendship with Baden-Powell continued and Baden-Powell, on retiring, came to Outspan and lived in his cottage, Paxtu, for the rest of his life. He died in 1941 and is buried there. His grave is a place of pilgrimage for Boy Scouts and Girl Guides worldwide.

Being a BOAC manager of a large airport overseas entailed many duties at any time of the day and night. Apart from being responsible for the aircraft and passengers passing through, departing and arriving at the airport, there were many other official duties and ad hoc events. On one occasion a member of staff from the UK was on honeymoon in Mombasa. Tragically he was drowned and it was Peter's job to make arrangements for his body to be flown home. We both flew down to Mombasa and whilst Peter was seeing to the official arrangements, I was in the hotel trying to console the bereaved widow. A large base overseas was in some ways like a big family, dealing with the difficult times as well as keeping all the members happy, entertaining visiting members and generally being on 24hr call.

The road from Nairobi to Mombasa follows the railway line which was built in dangerous conditions by the early European settlers, employing local workers. Wildlife, particularly lions, took their toll on the labourers as was vividly described by Col Patterson in his book 'The Man-Eaters of Tsavo'. Following the road south east from Nairobi to Mombasa the first port of call for all travellers was Hunter's Lodge. Continuing, the road divides Tsavo National Park into East and West. The nearest lodge to the West is Kilaguni where we stayed one night. Lots of elephants came to the pool to drink amongst the other wildlife. You can see Mount Kilimanjaro and visit Mzumi Springs, 8 miles away, where many hippos can be seen. We were back in Nairobi by early evening.

The following month we had another overnight trip to Tsavo but this time to the East. After visiting Hunter's Lodge we continued on the Mombasa Road. We called at the petrol station at Voi and discovered a choice of three 'loos'! Women, Men (long stay) and Men (short stay)! Continuing we then visited Mudando Rock – an outcrop of rock with a pool beneath. Here you can sit and watch herds of elephants come and go. They have a good wash and a long drink and go on their way. We stayed overnight at Salt Lick Lodge. Later on another occasion we visited Tsavo East again. This time we stayed at the Voi Safari Lodge. This lodge has wonderful views over the park and looks down on the watering hole. It was a popular spot because of its high standards and the wonderful viewing platform. It also had a well-known bar. One item, of many, on the cocktail menu is worth mentioning. It was called 'Hippopotamus for-a-lot-of us' consisting of rum, vodka, sherry, lime juice and sugar and served six people! Other cocktails of various ingredients had equally evocative names; Frog's Croak, Ostrich Kick, Red Elephant and Tsavo Sunset.

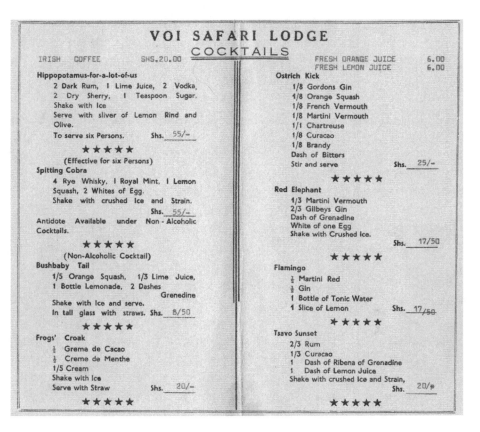

Voi Safari Lodge Cocktail List

It was probably just as well everyone was staying overnight! On our way home we went to see the Lugard Falls on the Galana River. They were discovered by Captain Lugard whilst exploring on behalf of the Imperial British East Africa Co. in 1890. At one point it flows through a ravine and standing on the edge looking down you can see very large crocodiles sunning themselves at the edge of the water.

The Ngong Hills lay to the west of Nairobi and were in 'Karen Blixen' (of Out of Africa fame) country – very atmospheric. It was here in the area of Nairobi called Karen, where we spent the last months of our posting. Windy Ridge was a development of lovely colonial type houses, each in their own 5 acre plot and we felt very privileged. Our house was called Ndege House … ndege being Swahili for bird.

This house was ideal for entertaining and on the Boxing Day of our last

Christmas there we held an open house for the other staff and two crews who were on a rest break. Over sixty people turned up with the crew arriving in coaches from the hotel! It was a beautiful spot surrounded by open country. We were quite near Langata Gate, one of the entrances to the Nairobi Game Park. Like most residents we took out an annual membership entitling us to to unlimited access to this fifty square miles of park. It also had a migration corridor to the Massai areas. Whenever we had a few hours to spare we would take advantage of this wonderful opportunity to watch the wild life. It was never very crowded and there was always the chance to see all of the native animals and birds, with the exception of elephants, in their natural surroundings. The park had several numbered areas and on entering the usual question was – where is the activity today? The reply would be something like, a pride of lions at No.8 or cheetahs seen near No.2, so off we would go armed with our map and camera. When we reached the relevant area we would often come across two or three other cars parked at a discreet distance from the animals.

Most people would have binoculars and would sit quietly watching any activity. Sometimes we would just drive around taking a chance on what we might see and would drive to less frequented parts where there were usually a multitude of smaller game and colourful birds. One of our favourites were little dik-diks, a small antelope just like Bambi! There were zebras, giraffe, wildebeest, ostriches and warthogs amongst many others. There was also the hippo pool where the hippos would wallow in the muddy waters while mischievous monkeys would climb all over your car at the slightest opportunity and woe betide you if you had left a window open! Occasionally a rhinoceros would lumber into view.

Visits to the game parks and other sightseeing trips consisted of a very small part of our time in Kenya, but were very memorable.

Chapter 19

Pakistan, Bahamas and Iran (1973 – 1975)

In July (1973) Peter left Nairobi and came home for a month's leave in our new home on Shoreham Beach, a week of which Peter spent in Putney Hospital having varicose veins sorted! He also had postings to Nassau then Abu Dhabi cancelled and eventually went to Karachi for 3 months at the end of August. Liz went back to school while Sue was at home waiting to start university at the beginning of October. She had a place at Guildford studying Hotel and Catering Management. A few days later I flew out to Karachi – I had a row of seats to myself and we stopped at Damascus and Kuwait for refuelling. Peter was staying in a company house in the west of the city. It was a very different area from the one I last visited twenty three years earlier in my flying days. Then we spent the night in an hotel in the centre of town surrounded by a bustling, overcrowded and poverty stricken population mostly living on the streets. It was quite awe-inspiring and I don't ever remember leaving the hotel.

But this time I saw a different side of the city. We had a temporary membership to the local expat sports and social club called the Boat Club, where we were regular visitors, but we were also invited to two Pakistani weddings.

For the first one we were sitting facing a brightly lit stage. There were rows of seats in the large courtyard of the hotel, enough to accommodate the 700-800 guests. Behind the chairs were more tables and chairs and huge buffet tables. It was warm, the sky was dark as it was the evening but the whole area was lit with coloured lights and the stage was beautifully decorated with white and silver-red flowers and green leaves. The atmosphere was very informal; women in gorgeous saris of bright and embroidered silks were moving amongst the more soberly dressed men-folk, greeting, talking and waiting. Then the music struck up the familiar, but rather incongruous, tune 'Here Comes the Bride' and coming down the 'aisle' between the rows of guests was the bride, on her father's arm, dressed in a white lace sari showing up beautifully against her black hair and dark skin. This was a Parsee wedding and the setting was an hotel in Karachi. There were about 5,000 Parsees living in this city, with the majority of this sect living in Bombay. They originally came from Persia and still had some traditions from that country, such as the girls being given Persian names. Light-skinned and hospitable they are a very close-knit group. Their natural language is Gujarati, but they spoke English extremely well.

The second wedding was similar – the Bride and Groom were seated on a 'stage' and all the guests lined up to ascend a few steps. As they passed the couple congratulating them and wishing them well, they pinned rupee notes to the bride's clothing. The unexpected musical accompaniment to this ceremony was Cliff Richards singing 'Congratulations'! As these were alcohol free occasions there was a special room set aside for European guests to slip into for a 'quick one'!

We went to Lake Kahri, about 80 miles to the east visiting various archaeological sites en route and then stopping for a picnic at the lake-side. Lake Kahri is connected to the River Indus and provided Karachi with much of its water. We also went to Hawkes Bay and Clifton Beach to the west, where you could go camel riding. On another day I won 75 rupees at Bingo at the Boat Club! After two weeks of living in another world I was back home, having flown back 1st class via Dubai and Beiruit.

Soon after returning, with Liz still at boarding school and Sue at university, I enrolled in an Interior Design correspondence course. Peter returned from Karachi but within two weeks we were back at the airport again as he was off to Nassau. I then spent the next few weeks preparing for Xmas, sending in my 'work' for my course and then at the beginning of December I was on a Jumbo to Nassau via Miami.

Peter was staying at Harbour Mews, an exclusive gated development of small houses with its own beach near to Cable Beach Hotel to the west of Nassau.

Nassau and its surroundings had been built up a lot since our last posting twenty odd years previously. It now, not only catered for the rich and independent winter visitor, but also for a new group of summer holiday makers that arrived by cruise ship or on a package holiday.

After being out there for a few days, I was not well and in a lot of pain. The doctor came to see me (the same ex-naval doctor who I saw 20 years previously!). Eventually I was rushed into hospital for an emergency operation 5 days before Christmas. I was released to go home on Christmas Day and poor Sue and Liz who had arrived a few days earlier had to cope not only with Christmas but me as well! They did a wonderful job and returned to school and university at the beginning of January.

Living in Harbour Mews we were able to use the facilities of Cable Beach Hotel. This included boat trips to a small island off shore then known as Balmoral Island but now called Discovery Island. We were able to take a picnic and swim from the almost deserted beach.

One of the other residents of Harbour Mews at this time was Max Bygraves and his wife known as Blossom. Peter, as was his custom with certain 'privileged persons', took them the latest English papers which arrived on the aircraft.

I gradually got stronger, but did not fully recover so came home in February. I returned to Nassau in April for a month, still doing my correspondence design course! Sue stayed in England during the summer working during her university break. Liz, however, came out for a holiday in the summer but was rather lonely until a school friend came to join her when they made full use of the neighbouring hotel pool and trips to the island.

Peter moved on to Freeport for a month and then returned home in January '75.

Peter was offered early retirement after a short trip to Teheran at the beginning of 1975. So we were house hunting again for a larger more permanent house which we could call 'home'. We viewed many possible homes over several weeks and months and were still looking when Peter left for Iran. What we really wanted was a house with some land as Peter was desperate to settle down and 'grow' things. Unfortunately in Sussex, prices ruled that out. However, as will be seen later fate was soon to take a part in achieving this.

I continued to make arrangements for selling the house, house hunting, doing my course, dressmaking and seeing friends and family. Liz and I flew out to join Peter for a week. Our visit was slightly different to the one that Sue had made several years previously. No helicopters or security guards or ultra-wealthy families for us! However we made the most of our stay.

Teheran had been the capital of Persia, then Iran, since the late 18C. The ruler at the time of our visit was still Shah Reza Pahlavi and he remained as Head of State until the revolution in 1979. Tehran lies at the southern edge of the Alborz mountain range and the company flat was to the north of the city so at the foot of this range, and was spacious and comfortable but well protected. The driving was really 'hairy' mostly by taxis who knew no rules of any road! The taxi drivers often drove under the influence of drink or drugs as we discovered on one journey as the driver had a roving hand as Liz reported when we arrived home!

We had several meals out during our stay, one memorable one with vodka, caviar and blinis. We also went to see the crown jewels; the quantity and richness of the stones was overwhelming with the centrepiece of the Peacock Throne in all its magnificence. After a week we were back home again and Peter soon followed marking the end of nearly 30 years of overseas postings.

Chapter 20

Retirement

We sold our house on Shoreham Beach and moved to Charmendean, an area to the north of Worthing and at the foot of the Downs. It had a small but magnificent garden full of azaleas which we discovered had been open to the public when the shrubs were in full bloom! For the first year we did the same, manning the entrance gate and collecting money for a nurses' charity.

The following year both Peter and I had 'jobs'! Mine was just 'one of those things'! Browsing in a small newly opened second-hand book shop in Worthing, the owner asked me if I would keep an eye on things whilst he 'nipped out'. It turned out that he was in the shop all day on his own so I offered to come in and work for a few hours each day. So I worked from 11-4 for the next few years. I was in my element surrounded by books and talking to people who were interested in them. But more important to our future was a by-product of Peter's little sinecure! The local bank had a small sub-branch in Findon (near Worthing) manned only by a cashier. For security and general reasons it was decided that it was advisable to have someone else around. So Peter applied and became the 'someone'! He would take the Daily Telegraph and read it cover to cover to while away the time. One day the Telegraph was on strike so a copy of the Daily Mail was delivered instead. Browsing through the adverts there was one that sounded interesting:-

"Smallholding with bungalow and two acres in Dorset."

It was only advertised the once and the owner turned out to be a reluctant seller. Anyway we arranged to stay at the Royal Chase in Shaftesbury for the weekend and collected details of other properties in the area to visit. None of the others were suitable, so we went to discover Little Homestead, Higher Langham being on the outskirts of

Gillingham. Nobody we asked seemed to have heard of Higher Langham and it took quite a while to finally locate it. We eventually arrived and discovered that this 2 acre plot was owned by a lady on crutches with a pet 3 'uddered' cow! Her surname turned out to be 'Little'. The bungalow was built in the 30's and the land was originally a chicken farm and was situated on the highest point to the west of Gillingham and had a magnificent unrestricted view over the Blackmore Vale. We decided that this was it and planned a second visit. This was facilitated by the fact that the Royal Chase had offered us a free country weekend! This came about because just prior to our first visit they had had fire doors fitted along the corridors. There was one outside our room and all through the night people were passing and the door noisily banged shut after them. We had complained and they agreed and offered us the complimentary visit!

So in August we started negotiations of buying and selling, but it wasn't until the following March we finally moved. It was a lovely sunny early spring day and here was I, after a very circuitous route, arriving in Dorset via many countries and adventures and a very full life. Now I was ready to settle down in one place but continue to have a very busy life.

Since retiring to Dorset I have had many interests and occupations. I built up a very small but flourishing second hand book business, was controller of the local W.I. market for a while, alongside visiting my mother, initially by commuting to Worthing and latterly to a local residential care home. We also continued with our travelling and exploring. I went back to Cairo twice (to visit Sue who was then working there) and we visited the Seychelles, Cape Town, Corfu, Lake Garda, Madrid and Portugal as well as numerous visits to France and Belgium.

Our daughters both have their own stories to tell – which I hope they will.

Sue went to University and then joined British Airways following in her father's footsteps as a duty officer then country manager at various overseas stations before working back in the UK. She now lives locally with her partner Mick and has helped me a lot, especially in the compilation of this book.

Liz took a different route and joined Beecham, a large pharmaceutical firm (later merging with Glaxo Wellcome to form GSK), where she worked for

26 years in a variety of roles. She is now happily married to Richard and lives and works in Devon.

Both have been very supportive over producing these memoirs.

Sadly Peter died in 2008.